Antique Tra

RADIO AND
TELEVISION

PRICE GUIDE

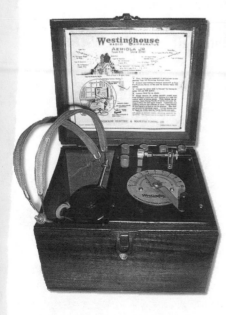

Edited by
Kyle Husfloen

Contributing Editors
Steve McVoy
Harry Poster
Bob Ready

©2005 KP Books
Published by

kp books
An Imprint of F+W Publications

700 East State Street • Iola, WI 54990-0001
715-445-2214 • 888-457-2873

Our toll-free number to place an order or obtain
a free catalog is (800) 258-0929.

Library of Congress Catalog Number: 2005906852
ISBN: 0-89689-133-X

Designed by Wendy Wendt
Edited by Kyle Husfloen

Printed in Canada

Collecting and Pricing Vintage Radios and Televisions

by Harry Poster

With the continued pressure of the online buyers from around the world, many of the well established collectible values of vintage radios and televisions have changed.

Radios and televisions that were super rare only a few years ago can now be found online, and their prices have dropped; other seemingly common sets have become of interest to many more collectors throughout the world, with a resulting escalation of their value.

Colorful Bakelite sets (also known as "Catalin") are still really hot, even when the cabinets are in less than perfect condition. And if you're a television collector, prewar TVs (those produced before 1940) are still as rare as ever, but because there are only a few collectors able—or

Classic FADA Model 1000 "Bullet" radio with deep maroon Catalin case, 1946, $1,250.

willing—to pay thousands of dollars for televisions, the less common prewars are now worth more, while the more common prewars have bottomed out in price. "Porthole" screen sets from the 1940s, those with completely round screens, early color TVs, and even some 1950s colorful metal portables have become popular.

Once you establish the vintage of your radio or TV, you should then be able to approximate a value. Sometimes radios and TVs made by the same manufacturer in the same model year will have vastly different values, so be sure to take into account the cosmetic condition,

The first mass-produced color television, RCA Model CT-100 color console model, 1954, $4,000.

Airite Model 4000 "inkstand" shape novelty radio, 1938, $250.

special styling, size, and composition before trying to establish a value.

The strangely designed 1950s Philco Predicta television sets, with an attached, moveable screen above, are still worth more than the typical rectangular shaped plastic Philco portables from the same period. The 1930s Emerson Mickey Mouse wooden radios are still worth considerably more than the typical square wooden sets from the same period. And a colorful Bakelite FADA tabletop radio from the 1930s or 1940s is worth significantly more than a wooden FADA tabletop from the same year.

Vintage Radios: Estimating Collectible Values

First, check the case to establish its condition and composition. Cabinets from the 1920s and 1930s were often made of wood or a wood composition material, the earliest with black Bakelite panels; inside these early radios there is usually one or more vacuum tubes. Radios from the 1920s and 1930s were often table sets, but some portables and consoles were also manufactured. Larger sets made from the 1920s to early 1930s followed the lines of Depression furniture; smaller sets were very square-cornered, with large internal components, usually separated, and wired point to point.

Asymmetrically designed sets, radios with chrome parts,

Meissner Model 10-1153, metal kit TV with no cabinet, 1939, $4,500.

Stewart Warner Model A6S, featuring Bakelite case decorated with images of the Dionne Quintuplets, 1930s, $150.

and those with mirrors applied to the sides or front of the cases were occasionally produced in the 1930s and 1940s. Console and tabletop sets from the late 1930s through the 1940s often have an Art Deco look, with curved or inlaid designs. Post-World War II consoles usually have square lines, with many having the features of typical period buffets. Some of these radios will have several short-wave bands as well as the standard band or AM radio band, while even more modern sets, from the 1950s and later, will be marked with FM and often hi-fi or stereo.

Some radios were made entirely of Bakelite by 1930, and these early plastic sets can be found through the 1960s. Some of the Bakelite radios from the 1950s and 1960s were often painted over to change the original brown or black to a more pleasing color. Colored Bakelite, as opposed to painted black Bakelite or "Catalin" cabinets,

are very thick, poured, and semi-translucent, with the same bright color throughout.

Inside the radio, the electronic components can help you determine the approximate vintage. Some of the first radio sets in the teens and 1920s have a small metal holder with a chip inside the case or mounted on the front with a "cat's whisker" wire, which functioned as the tuner. Usually these crystal sets are simple, built on or in plain wooden cases, and have few components. They are desirable, even when the set was a "home-brew" product rather than a mass-produced set.

Vacuum tubes from the 1920s and 1930s were rather large, about the size of a 15-watt lightbulb. These usually had Bakelite bases with four, five, or six pins. The radios often had one to seven tubes within the

RCA Model 66X1 with dark Bakelite case, 1946, $45.

cabinet, with one or more of the vacuum tubes having a metal cap with an insulated wire running down from the top. Numbers like 01A, 80, 71A, 230, 380 and similar are found on the tubes from this period. By the 1940s, most vacuum tubes were smaller, about the size of a finger, with eight pins in a Bakelite base, and some tubes might be smaller yet, with the metal pins brought directly out of the glass base. Numbers like 6AU6, 7C7, 12AT6, 35Z5 are common. Later 1950s and 1960s

This Crosley brochure from the 1950s promises "The most colorful radios in the world." Shown below is the brochure unfolded to reveal the models available: clock radios, "clock-radio-phono combination" models, and portable radios, all in striking colors and bold designs.

Admiral
Model 19A1,
tabletop model
in Bakelite
case with
checkerboard
grill, 1948, $150.

tube-type sets had printed circuit boards with components mounted onto these boards, including the smaller peanut-sized tubes.

If the set has Civil Defense markings on the AM dial, it was probably made in the period from World War II until the early 1960s. Regency introduced the first all-transistor radio, and most small pocket-sized U.S. or Japanese transistor sets with an AM band that have Civil Defense markings will date from about 1955 to 1962. Earlier transistor sets usually have rounded corners and are often made of soft plastic or nylon. Hard plastic cases with square corners usually date from the late 1960s or even later.

Vintage Televisions: Estimating Collectible Values

Although it's a surprise to many beginning collectors, the pioneering years of television were very early in the 20th century, and many TV sets were actually produced in the 1920s and early 1930s. These earliest of TVs were basically a wooden box with glass lens through which the user could see an image produced by a perforated spinning metal or paper disc spun by a motor. These mechanical-type "televisors" were

Emerson Model 508,
console model with
pop-up screen, late-
1940s, $350.

"scanning disc sets." Surprisingly, they often command less money than other TVs from the later 1930s, since the scanners cannot easily be made to work.

By the late 1930s, RCA, GE and several other companies sold TVs to the public, and many magazines advertised kits that allowed radio hobbyists to actually build their own TV receivers. The 1939 World's Fair was one of the first large-scale public venues where TVs were displayed and sold. RCA sold more than 1,000 mirror-in-the-lid sets in 1939 and 1940, many as a result of the public's notice of the industry at the World's Fair.

These late-1930s TV sets have a five- to 20-inch-long funnel-shaped picture tube, a tuner with five or fewer channels (channels 6 through 13 didn't exist), and a deadly high voltage supply inside. Both tabletops and consoles were produced, and the TV kits offered models either with or without cabinets.

By the mid-1940s, seven-inch portable TVs and tabletops and consoles with 10-15-inch screen sizes were available. By 1950, 16-inch black-and-white tubes were common, and soon after, DuMont, a wartime contractor and TV set manufacturer, was able to produce a 30-inch black-and-white television set.

Many 1950s TVs were mass-produced, with a minimum of detailing, and by the mid-1950s many televisions included UHF as well as the standard VHF stations. Fifteen-inch color TVs were sold in 1954 by both Westinghouse and RCA, and the RCA CT-100 has become very popular with collectors. By 1955 the 21-inch round color tubes were produced, and many makers incorporated these "large" color tubes in their sets.

Harry Poster has been collecting and dealing in radios and vintage TVs since 1982. He travels to radio meets and antiques shows across the country. He also buys and sells both radios and TVs mail-order across the country and around the world. His illustrated price guide, Poster's Radio and Television Price Guide, *is out of print, but to ascertain the approximate value of your vintage radio or television, e-mail him at hposter@att.net with its description, a JPG or TIFF image, if available, and your location. Or visit his Web site at http://www. harryposter.com to check on the current stock or just to reminisce. If you prefer, you can send a written description, photo and other information, in-cluding the location of the set, with a self-addressed stamped envelope to: Harry Poster, PO Box 1883, So. Hackensack, NJ 07606.*

Panasonic Model TR-005, "Flying Saucer" model, 1971, $375.

A WORD TO THE READER

Having come into the world in 1949, in the early years of the Baby Boomer Explosion, my earliest memories of electronic entertainment include that pivotal period when radio was dying out and television was burgeoning. Although still a preschooler I can remember accompanying my Dad when we went to pick up the slightly used television from a nearby couple. It wasn't JUST a TV but a whole 'entertainment center,' with a phonograph and radio all included in the handsome blond mahogany two-door cabinet. The first night we plugged it in we didn't even have the antenna up, but I sat and "listened" to my first episode of *Dragnet* through the 'snow' on the screen.

At the same time that television was becoming a big part of my young life I did, of course, still listen to the radio and loved the Pop music of the 1950s. Actual 'programming' on radio was pretty much at an end but I do recall one Saturday morning radio show for kids that used the "Teddy Bears' Picnic" as the theme song. Also, about 1960, my folks passed along to me the big old wooden tabletop radio that had belonged to my grandfather in the 1940s. The neatest part was that it had a big short wave dial and sometimes my brother and I could pick-up nighttime broadcasts from Hawaii or the Far East right in our bedroom. As late as 1964 this trusty old set was still working perfectly and I can recall hearing on it the first news reports of the horrific Alaska earthquake that year.

Although both these trusty machines of my youth are long gone I'm sure many folks of my generation have similar memories of the wonderful sounds and sites they brought into our young lives. After reviewing all the great listings in this new price guide my only disappointment is that probably NEITHER of my treasured broadcasting friends would sell for much more than $100 today.

Putting together the *Antique Trader Radio & Television Price Guide* has been a wonderful learning experience for me. I was somewhat familiar with the values of some of the classic 1920s and 1930s radios and knew that rare pre-1940s televisions should be 'valuable.' What I learned, and you the reader will also learn, is what other sets are really collectible and pricey and how many are still very modestly priced. As is to be expected, radios or TVs with unique styling of the cases or innovative technological features will have the strongest collector appeal. I also can understand why space limitations would make tabletop TVs of more interest than most console models, no matter how elegant their wood cabinets are.

Our new price guide is divided into the two main categories, Radios and Televisions, and then the pieces are listed alphabetically by the name of the manufacturer. We also have been able to include a selection of early vintage Microphones in our listings since they were such an important part of early broadcasting history. We are especially pleased to be able to include hundreds of photographs, ALL in color, which makes it so much easier to appreciate the design details of each piece.

This new price guide would not have been possible without the unselfish assistance of a number of experts and I must thank them here.

I have had the pleasuring of working with Harry Poster for a number of years and he was always generous with listings on vintage radios and televisions. He stepped forward again here and did some monumental work for me.

In spite of health problems, Bob Ready made Herculean efforts to also obtain for me a wide selection of great radios as well as the microphones. He deserves a real rest now that the heavy labor is over.

Work was well underway on this guide when I made a very fortuitous contact with Kevin Gretsch, an advanced collector of radios who stepped in and presented me with even more wonderful radio listings and photos. His Web site offers a wonderful opportunity to see the vast treasure trove that forms his collection.

Finally, a truly huge thank you must go out to Steve McVoy. Without his generosity and hard work I wouldn't be able to show you nearly as many vintage Televisions as we now have available. His detailed information on each set and the fine quality of his images highlight our comprehensive Televisions section. Steve was also provided with images from Sonny Clutter, Chuck Azzalina, David Bertinot and Fred Hoffman while Tom Genova and Chuck Azzalina assisted him with the pricing of the pieces.

For further information:

Harry Poster
P.O. Box 1883
So. Hackensack, NJ 07606

Bob Ready
7088 W. Jefferson Dr.
Mentor, OH 44060
e-mail: HYPERLINK "mailto:
   bradioready63@aol.com"
   bradioready63@aol.com

Kevin Gretsch
e-mail: HYPERLINK "mailto:
   mrkevo4@earthlink.net"
   mrkevo4@earthlink.net
Web: Search "Allen's Radio City"

Steve McVoy
4350 Dublin Rd.
Columbus, OH 43221
e-mail: HYPERLINK "mailto:
   etf@columbus.rr.com" etf@columbus.
   rr.com
Web: HYPERLINK "http://www.ear-
   lytelevision.org" www.earlytelevision.
   org

Kyle Husfloen
Editor

PART 1

Radios

A.C. Dayton, Model R-12, large wooden set w/Bakelite panel, mid-1920s $100

Addison, Model 2A, white Bakelite case $550

Addison, Model 2A, yellow & burgundy Bakelite, Art Deco design........................ $2,000

Admiral, Model 34F5, portable, leatherette case w/decorative grille, 1940s $25

Admiral, Model 4-A-15, AM/FM console, ca. 1948... $40

Admiral, Model 4X11, plastic portable model, 1950s.. $40

Admiral, Model 5A32, clock radio, brown or white, each.. $30

Admiral, Model 5D32, radio-phonograph in a low rectangular black Bakelite case, dial, knobs & speaker at the front, 1953 (ILLUS., bottom of page) $75-100

Admiral, Model 5M21, Bakelite, radio/phonograph, large... $55

Admiral, Model 5X12, plastic, tabletop, late 1940s $35

Admiral, Model 5X12, tabletop model in painted Bakelite case, ca. 1948 .... $15

Admiral, Model 5Y22, oversized radio-phonograph tabletop model in brown Bakelite $30

Admiral, Model 6P32, leatherette, portable, 1940s $35

Admiral, Model 742, leather-covered tube-type portable w/carrying handle on top, 1960 .... $10

Admiral, Model AZ593, "farm" set, portable, takes 6-volt battery, ca. 1938...................... $35

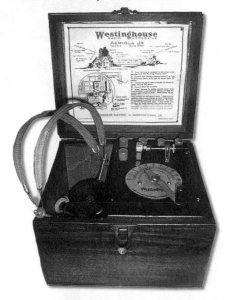

1922 Aeriola, Jr. Crystal Radio Set

Aeriola, Jr., crystal set in wooden case w/hinged cover, w/earphones, 1922 (ILLUS.).. $350

Admiral Model 5D32 Bakelite Radio-Phonograph

Air Castle Streamlined Radio-Phonograph

Aeriola, Sr. One-tube 1922 Receiver Set

Air Castle, Model 935, Bakelite, tabletop, 1940s **$45**

Air Chief, Model 4-A-24, simple wooden tabletop model w/AM-FM, 1940s **$30**

Air King, Model 5000, leatherette, portable, 1940s **$45**

Air King, Model 52, classic "skyscraper" style in white Bakelite, 1933.................... **$3,500**

Air King, Model 66, Bakelite, "skyscraper" w/clock, white, 1933................................ **$4,500**

Aeriola, Sr., one-tube battery receiver in wooden case w/hinged cover, 1922 (ILLUS.)... **$250**

Air Castle, Model 302, radio-phonograph in metal case resembling the front end of a sporty car, open turntable on the top, creamy white color, 1941 (ILLUS., top of page)... **$175-225**

Air Castle, Model 5012, wooden, tombstone-shaped, tabletop, 1930s.................... **$85**

Air Castle, Model 5027, large wooden portable w/three small knobs on the front & carrying handle on the top, 1946.................. **$10**

Unusual Air King Camera-Radio in Case

Air King, Model A-410, camera-radio, wooden case w/faux reptile skin carrying case, battery-operated, 1948 (ILLUS.) **$100-150**

Airite Inkstand Novelty Radio

Air King, Model A-510, portable, leatherette case... **$25**

Air King, Model A-600, Catalin, green & yellow, 1947... **$1,200**

Airite, Model 4000, inkstand-style novelty radio, thin Bakelite case, 1938 (ILLUS., top of page)... **$250**

Airline, Model 64-BR-1208, wooden table-top set w/long AM/FM dial across the front, 1945.. **$25**

Airline, Model 74KR-2713, console model radio w/pull-out phonograph in a simple square style wooden cabinet, 1948 .... **$15**

Airline, Model 84BR1507, plastic case w/a half-moon dial on the front right & horizontal grille bars on the left, six pushbuttons, one front & one side knob, broadcast band, six-tubes, AC/DC, 1948 (ILLUS., bottom of page)..................... **$100-115**

Airline Model 84BR1507 Radio

Airline Model 93BR 462A Bakelite Radio

Airline, Model 93BR 462A, streamlined Art Deco brown Bakelite case w/louvers at one end, battery-powered, AM, 1939(ILLUS.) **$65-95**

Airline 1949 Plastic Table Model Radio

Airline, Model 94BR-1525A, plastic table model w/upper slide rule dial, lower horizontal wrap-around louvers, two bullet knobs, broadcast band, five tubes, AC/DC, 1949 (ILLUS.).. **$35-45**

Airline 1949 AM/FM Radio in Bakelite Case

Scarce AK Model 10C Five-tube Battery Receiver Set from 1924

Airline, Model 94BR-1535A, stepped rect-angular black Bakelite case, AM/FM, wide arched grille across the top front, 1949 (ILLUS.)... **$35-50**

Airline, Model 94WG-2740 large wooden console model w/built-in phonograph that pulls out, ca. 1947.. **$25**

AK, Model 10C, five-tube breadboard bat-tery receiver on mahogany base, 1924 (ILLUS., middle from top)........................... **$950**

AMC, table model in dark yellow Catalin drop-handle case, wide band of louvers across the front, similar to Garod Model 1B55L, 1940s (ILLUS., top next page) **$2,000**

Amrad Neutrodyne, crystal set, wooden case, five or seven tubes, 1920, each **$150**

Arvin, Model 240-P, four-tube portable in a plastic case w/a rounded design **$15**

Arvin, Model 2572, five-tube plastic table model, ca. 1962 .... **$10**

Arvin, Model 302A, streamlined painted Bakelite radio-phonograph, 1940s............... **$45**

AMC Radio in Catalin Case

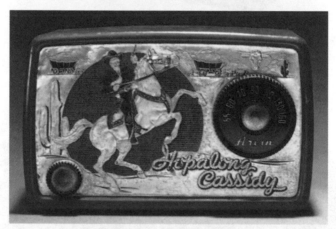

Arvin Hopalong Cassidy Radio

Arvin Model 444A Midget Style Radio

Atwater Kent Radio & Phonograph

Arvin, Model 441-T, Hopalong Cassidy metal tabletop model in red & silver (ILLUS., middle previous page).................. **$650**

Arvin, Model 444A, Midget style metal case w/right front dial, horizontal louvers, raised top, two knobs, broadcast band, four tubes, AC/DC, 1946 (ILLUS., bottom previous page) **$80-90**

Arvin, Model 532, Catalin set, yellow & brown, 1930s.. **$2,000**

Arvin, Model 532, maroon Catalin w/yellow trim, 1930s **$2,000**

Arvin, Model 850T, painted plastic, 1950s **$435**

Arvin, tabletop tube-type clock-radio in a wide case w/stylish trim, early 1960s........... **$45**

Atwater Kent, floor model radio/phonograph, wooden case w/elaborate scrolling, phonograph hidden by wood sliding doors (ILLUS., top of page)....................... **$300**

Atwater Kent, Kiel table model w/six legs, top exposing radio inside **$350**

Atwater Kent, Model 10, breadboard style, exposed controls & tubes....................... **$1,250**

Atwater Kent, Model 20C, crystal set in a simple wide wooden tabletop case, 1920s **$75**

Atwater Kent, Model 441, simple metal tabletop model, late 1920s............................. **$85**

Atwater Kent Model 45 Radio

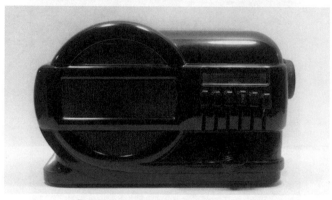

Belmont Model 519 Streamlined Radio

Streamlined Belmont Model 60111 Radio from 1946

Atwater Kent, Model 45, low rectangular green & black metal cabinet, 1925 (ILLUS., top of page).................................... **$65**

Atwater Kent, wooden table model, Cathedral styling, early 1930s, also known as "midget" or "Depression" models, price depends on the company, several variations of style found .... **$150+**

Belmont, Model 519, brown plastic streamlined case, the dial on the front right, the left w/a circular grille w/horizontal bars, six pushbuttons, one front & one right side knob, broadcast band, five tubes, AC/DC, 1939 (ILLUS., middle of page) **$170-190**

Streamlined Belmont Model 6D-111 Radio

Belmont, Model 60111, oblong streamlined creamy white Bakelite case w/rounded ends, 1946 (ILLUS., bottom previous page) **$100-150**

Belmont, Model 6D-111, plastic streamlined, the right front half w/a round dial, the left side w/horizontal grille bars, six pushbuttons, one front & one right side knob, broadcast band, six tubes, AC/DC, 1946 (ILLUS., top of page) **$140-170**

Belmont, Model 6D-120, Bakelite, streamlined style, ca. 1940s **$155**

Belmont, Model 6D-128, streamlined painted Bakelite case **$135**

Bendix, Model 0526C, thin plastic tan & brown case **$250**

Bendix, Model 0626A, painted Bakelite white case **$55**

Bendix, Model 0626A, tabletop model in a painted Bakelite case w/three knobs near the bottom, 1946 .... **$30**

Bendix, Model 301, wooden tabletop model, ca. 1949 .... **$35**

Bendix, Model 526C, Catalin case in green w/black trim, upper front slide rule dial, lower horizontal louvers, two knobs, broadcast band, five tubes, AC/DC, 1946 (ILLUS., bottom of page) **$650-850**

Bendix, tube-type table model in a plastic case w/a long dial above an oversized grille, ca. 1946 .... **$10**

Fine Catalin Bendix Model 526C Radio

Brewster Model 9-1084 with Unusual Case

Brewster, Model 9-1084, rectangular dark brown plastic case w/a recessed right side w/slide rule dial, the left side w/horizontal bars, step-down rectangular top, three knobs, broadcast band, five watts, six tubes, 1946 (ILLUS., top of page)...... **$50-60**

Capehart, Model 1P55, plastic portable model w/a large center dial, four-tube set, mid-1950s **$45**

Capehart, Model 1P55, plastic portable style w/handle **$20**

Capehart, Model T-522, plastic tabletop model, 1950s.. **$25**

Channel Master, Model 6506, small tabletop radio **$45**

Colonial, New World Globe model, novelty Bakelite style, 1930s................................. **$850**

Continental, Model 738-44, bullet-shaped plastic tabletop model, ca. 1955 .... **$25**

Coronado, Model 8351, Bakelite tabletop model w/two knobs & pushbuttons near the bottom, 1946.. **$35**

Crosley, Model 10-137, creamy white plastic case w/front center round dial w/inner perforated grille, two knobs, broadcast band, five tubes, AC/DC, 1950 (ILLUS., bottom of page).................................. **$100-120**

Crosley, Model 11-104, streamlined Bakelite case w/large central tuner & dial, 1950 .... **$95**

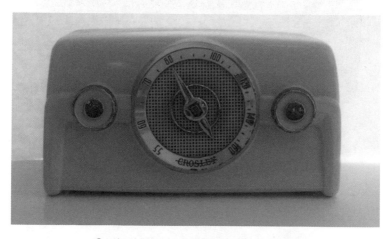

Crosley Model 10-137 White Plastic Radio

1951 Crosley Model 11-126 AM/FM Radio

Crosley, Model 11-126, dark brown Bakelite case w/large round gold speaker, AM/FM, 1951 (ILLUS., top of page) **$35-50**

Crosley, Model 11-207, curved-front wooden radio-phonograph w/large vertical speaker grille bars, ca. 1950 .... **$35**

Crosley, Model 122 "Super Buddy Boy" model, arched Repwood case w/molded leaf bands, AM, 1931 (ILLUS., bottom of page) **$350-500**

Crosley Model 122 "Super Buddy Boy" Radio

Crosley Model 15-WE Streamlined Radio from 1953

Crosley, Model 15-WE, white Bakelite streamlined case, 1953 (ILLUS.) **$75-100**

Crosley Model 48 "Wigit" Decorative Radio

Crosley, Model 48 "Wigit," arched Repwood case w/molded leafy scrolls, AM, 1931 (ILLUS.) **$300-400**

1920s Crosley Model 50 One-tube Radio

Crosley, Model 50, early one-tube tabletop radio, wooden case w/large metal front w/dials, 1925 (ILLUS., top of page)............ **$125**
Crosley, Model 50, early two-tube crystal radio **$175**

Crosley, Model 51, crystal set, two-tube battery model in wooden case, 1924 (ILLUS., bottom of page).................... **$150-200**

Crosley Model 51 Two-tube Battery Model Set from 1924

Fancy Crosley Model 54 "New Buddy" from 1930

Crosley, Model 54, "New Buddy," Repwood case w/ornate flowering scroll front design around & below the speaker, 1930 (ILLUS.) **$200-250**

Crosley "Duette" Model 1947 Radio

Crosley, Model 56-TD "Duette," high rounded dark brown plastic case w/slide rule dial, lower tall tan vertical bars, three knobs, broadcast band, five tubes, 1947 (ILLUS.).. **$110-150**

Art Deco Crosley Model 58 "Buddy Boy" Model Radio from 1931

Crosley, Model 56TU, painted Bakelite tabletop case, ca. 1940s **$65**

Crosley, Model 58, "Buddy Boy," Repwood arched case w/Art Deco style floral & scroll banded front around the speaker, 1931 (ILLUS., top of page)................. **$250-300**

Crosley, Model 628B, high gently arched & stepped black Bakelite case, AM/SW, 1939 (ILLUS., bottom of page)............. **$75-100**

Crosley, Model 66CS, wooden console model w/phonograph, 1940s........................ **$35**

Crosley Model 628B Bakelite Radio from 1939

Crosley Model 719A "Magnetune" Radio with Pushbutton Tuning

Crosley, Model 719A "Magnetune," dark brown Bakelite case w/magnetic push-button tuning, AM, 1940 (ILLUS., top of page) **$50-75**

Crosley, Model 88TC, tube-type wooden ta-bletop model, ca. 1946 .... **$15**

Crosley, Model 9-102, simple Bakelite tabletop model **$30**

Crosley, Model 9-113, plastic tabletop mod-el, 1949 .... **$20**

Crosley, Model 9-205M, console radio w/phonograph, 1950 .... **$35**

Crosley, Model 9-214, AM/FM console model w/phonograph **$45**

Crosley, Model D-10RD "Bull's-eye," red plastic case w/large center round dial w/inner circular louvers, fins at ends, two knobs, 1951 (ILLUS., bottom of page) **$140-170**

Red Crosley "Bull's-eye" Radio

Crosley 1953 Table Model Radio

Crosley, Model D-25TN, table model alarm clock-radio in a tan plastic case w/two small dials for control & two large dials above, one containing clock, the second for station control, 1953, 4 x 6 1/2 x 8" (ILLUS., top of page)........................... **$110-140**

Crosley, Model F-5 "Musical Chief" model, plastic case **$35**

Crosley, Pup model, small square metal case w/tube in top **$250**

Dahlberg, Model 430-DI, plastic coin-operated radio w/pillow-style speaker, 1955 (ILLUS., bottom of page).................... **$100-150**

Dahlberg Model 430-DI Plastic Coin-operated Radio

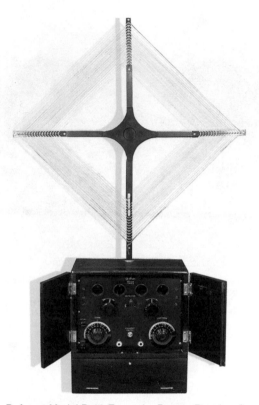

Early Deforest Model D-10 Four-tube Battery Receiver from 1923

Deforest, Model D-10, four-tube battery receiver in wooden case w/hinged doors &
loop antenna on top, 1923 (ILLUS., top of
page).. **$850**

Detrola, Model 576-1-6, wooden miniature
console-shaped tabletop model **$75**

Dewald, Model 502-A, tabletop model
w/clock, yellow Catalin case **$550**

Dewald, Model A-501, "Harp" style brown
Catalin case, upper front w/slide rule dial,
lower cloth grille w/five vertical bars, two
knobs, five tubes, BC, AC/DC, 1946
(ILLUS., bottom of page) **$600-650**

Dewald Model A-501 "Harp" Case Radio

Unusual English EKCO Upright Round Radio

EKCO, Model AD36, upright doughnut-shaped brown Bakelite case w/central speaker, AM/LW, England, 1935 (ILLUS., top of page)........................... **$600-850**

Electromatic, Model 512, radio-phonograph in a stepped & rounded bentwood cabinet raised on flat bentwood legs, 1946 (ILLUS., bottom of page)............ **$100-150**

Emerson, "Baby" model, one-tube, 1920s, complete **$650**

Emerson, clock-radio, 1950s, various models w/wake-up control **$20**

Electromatic Bentwood Radio-Phonograph

Emerson Model 400 "Aristocrat"

Emerson, Model 400 "Aristocrat," dark brown Catalin case w/white speaker bars & large dial, 1940 (ILLUS., top of page) **$500-600**

Emerson, Model 410, wooden case w/Mickey Mouse character decoration, 1930s **$2,000**

Emerson, Model 427, large portable style, cloth-covered w/handle, early 1940s **$60**

Emerson, Model 520, white & brown Catalin tabletop model, round dial on the right front, white panel w/checkered grille, two knobs, broadcast band, five tubes, AC/DC, 1946 (ILLUS., bottom of page) **$170-190**

Emerson, Model 539, wooden tabletop model, mid-1940s **$20**

Emerson, Model 575, plastic portable model, ca. 1950 .... **$20**

Emerson Model 520 in White & Brown Catalin Case

Emerson Model 581-A 1949 Plastic Radio

Emerson, Model 581-A, rectangular white plastic case w/a right front round dial over horizontal wrap-around grille bars, top handle, two knobs, broadcast band, five tubes, AC/DC, 1949 (ILLUS., top of page).. **$40-50**

Emerson, Model 868, Magic Wand antenna, portable, 1950s **$50**

Emerson, Model AU-190, tabletop style, blue Catalin case.................................... **$3,500**

Emerson, Model AX-235, small green Catalin case... **$2,500**

Emerson, Model Q-236, Snow White & the Seven Dwarfs radio, painted pressed Syroco wood upright case, molded w/a scene of Snow White dancing w/four Dwarfs before an open window flanked by shutters, Dwarfs Doc & Grumpy look out from the window while Dopey peers from behind the top of one shutter, stamped "Emerson" above the window, maker's plate on the back, turning knob in center of window w/selection numbers notched around the window edges, 1939, works perfectly, 5 1/2 x 7 1/4 x 7 1/2" (ILLUS., bottom of page)...................... **$2,000+**

Emud, Model 914, wooden console in a tall glossy cabinet, on four legs & w/swing-out speakers, ca. 1961.............................. **$225**

FADA, Model 10, wide wooden tabletop model, late 1920s...................................... **$100**

FADA, Model 1000, bullet-style, streamlined all-yellow or pumpkin Catalin case w/rounded end enclosing the dial, 1946, each **$950**

Emerson Snow White & Seven Dwarfs Radio

FADA Model 1000 in Dark Yellow & Orange

FADA, Model 1000, bullet-style, stream-lined dark yellow case w/dark orange knobs & the rounded end enclosing the dark orange ring around the dial, 1946 (ILLUS., top of page)................................... **$950**

FADA, Model 1000, bullet-style, stream-lined deep maroon Catalin case w/round-ed end enclosing the dial, 1946 (ILLUS., bottom of page).. **$1,250**

FADA, Model 1001, wooden, tabletop, ca. 1949 .... **$35**

FADA, Model 189, bullet-style in red, white & blue, all original & mint......................... **$4,000**

FADA, Model 5F-50, yellow Catalin case, square dial **$1,000**

FADA, Model 652, Temple-style tabletop model in blue Catalin, mint condition **$1,850**

FADA, Model 711, gold Catalin case, round dial **$350**

FADA, Model 845, plastic, "Cloud," tabletop **$150**

FADA, Model P-100, portable w/alligator leatherette case, 1940s............................... **$35**

FADA, Model P111, tube-type portable in a square case, AC/DC, ca. 1952 .... **$15**

FADA, Model P80, portable, late 1940s........... **$75**

FADA Bullet-style Catalin Radio

FADA Model R60 Radio with Aerial Inside

FADA, Model R60, wooden case w/gold dials for tuning & volume, w/fold-out aerial inside, six-tube battery set, ca. 1926, 25 x 13 1/2 x 11" (ILLUS.) **$90**

Firestone "Newscaster" Model Radio from 1948

Firestone, Model 4-A-26 "Newscaster," white rectangular plastic case w/slanted upper front w/slide rule dial above lower horizontal louvers, two knobs, broadcast band, five tubes, AC/DC, 1948 (ILLUS.)....... **$35-45**

Garod Model 5A4 "Thriftee" 1948 Radio

Garod, Model 5A4 "Thriftee," white plastic w/rounded top corners & upper slanted front slide rule dial, lower horizontal wrap-around grille bars, two knobs, broadcast band, five tubes, 1948 (ILLUS.) **$40-50**

General Electric Floor Model Radio

General Electric, Art Deco wooden floor model, clean w/original mask & knobs, 1939, 30 x 15 x 41" (ILLUS.)
.... **$95**

General Electric Model H-520 with Machine Age Styling

General Electric, Model 354, wooden console radio-phonograph w/a door in front of the radio & a pull-out phonograph, 1946 .... **$25**

General Electric, Model 410, wooden AM/FM tabletop model **$25**

General Electric, Model 50B, plastic clock radio, unbroken **$45**

General Electric, Model 511, plastic clock radio, ca. 1950 .... **$35**

General Electric, Model 605, simple plastic portable model **$40**

General Electric, Model 670, plastic portable, 1950s.. **$20**

General Electric, Model H-520, streamlined Machine Age styling in dark brown Bakelite, 1939 (ILLUS., top of page) **$150-200**

General Electric, Model H-610, rounded brown Bakelite case w/square dial at one end, 1939 (ILLUS., bottom of page) **$50-75**

General Electric, Model H-87, Art Deco-style console model, 1939 .... **$150**

General Electric, Models 412, 413 and 414, wide plastic tabletop model w/a large dial at the right, 1952, each................. **$15**

General Electric Model H-610 Bakelite Radio from 1939

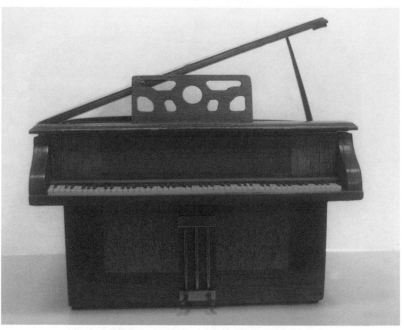

General Television "Grand Piano" Radio

General Television, Model 534 "Grand Piano," wooden model of a grand piano, an inner right dial, left G-clef grille, lift top, two knobs, broadcast band, five tubes, AC/DC, 1939 (ILLUS., top of page)..... **$300-350**

Grebe, Model CR18, two-tube battery receiver in quarter-sawn oak case, 1926 (ILLUS., bottom of page)......................... **$2,000**

Grundig Majestic, Model 4192, tabletop set in a wide & tall polished wood cabinet, ca. 1962.. **$85**

Guild, "Country Belle" model made to resemble an early wooden wall phone w/crank handle, ca. 1955............................ **$35**

Guild, Model 38CT, "Town Crier" model made to resemble a tall early lantern, tube-type, ca. 1955 .... **$55**

Kadette, Junior model, tall brown Bakelite case, two-tube portable model, 1930s....... **$375**

Kadette (International), Model K15, green classic oversized table model **$1,000**

Rare Grebe Model CR18 Two-tube Battery Receiver

Kadette Model KRC-2 "Tunemaster" Wooden Radio

Kadette (International), Model KRC-2 "Tunemaster," tall narrow oblong wooden case w/a stepped top & a large dial at one end, Universal remote control, 1939 (ILLUS., top of page)............................ **$100-150**

Kadette (International), Model L25, Topper Bakelite set w/unusual round grille at top, mint **$850**

Lamp radio, novelty-type, domed metal shade & trumpet-form shaft on a stepped round base fitted w/the speaker, dial & works, 1938 (ILLUS., bottom of page) **$225-275**

Unique Metal Novelty Lamp Radio

Majestic "Charlie McCarthy" Radio

Majestic, "Charlie McCarthy (The)," table model, white Bakelite, w/Charlie McCarthy figure on front of radio, 1930s (ILLUS.) **$950**

Majestic "Hospital" Model Tabletop Radio

Majestic, Model 15A410, "hospital" model, white plastic case w/raised slide rule dial on the upper front, lower horizontal wrap-around louvers, two knobs, broadcast band, 1946 (ILLUS.) **$80**

Mantola Model R-654-PV Ivory Plastic Radio

Early Masterdine Tabletop Radio

Mantola, Model R-654-PV, rectangular ivory plastic case, the upper front w/a slide rule dial, lower horizontal louvers, two knobs, broadcast band, five tubes, 1946 (ILLUS., top of page) **$35-45**

Marconi, six-tube table model, three bands, w/large fabric speaker on side, 1930s, 22 x 10 x 13" **$200**

Masterdine, early low rectangular tabletop model w/Bakelite front w/three large dials, by Mifflinburg Radio (ILLUS., second from top)... **$90**

Microphone radio, novelty-type, plastic, 1951 (ILLUS., next column) **$100-150**

Novelty Figural Microphone Radio

Mitchell "Lumitone" Table Lamp-Radio

Mitchell, "Lumitone" tabletop lamp-radio, white plastic bullet-shaped case, lower thumbwheel dial, upper horizontal grille bars, AC, 1940 (ILLUS., previous column)... $200

Mitchell, Model 1251 or 1261, hanging bed-lamp radio w/two knobs & a light bulb, ca. 1954, each $25

Motorola, Model 50XC2, "Circle Grille" Catalin case in turquoise blue w/yellow trim $3,000

Motorola, Model 51A, dark brown Bakelite case w/a large raised shield-form graduated speaker grille at one side, AM, 1939 (ILLUS., bottom of page).................... $100-150

Motorola, Model 51X16, "S-Grille" Catalin case in yellow w/green trim..................... $2,500

Motorola Model 51A Brown Bakelite Radio with Large Speaker Grille

Motorola Art Deco Style 1939 Plastic Radio

Motorola, Model 53C, creamy white plastic Art Deco style case w/a rectangular right front dial & a large raised grille on the left composed of graduated horizontal louvers, two knobs, broadcast band, five tubes, AC/DC, 1939 (ILLUS., top of page) **$70-80**

Motorola, Model 57CD, four-tube plastic tabletop clock-radio available in stylish colors, 1957 .... **$45**

Motorola, Model 57CE, simple plastic clock radio w/large square dial at the right **$15**

Motorola, Model 57W, blond wood tabletop model, 1957 .... **$25**

Motorola, Model 57W, tube-type model w/a long simple wooden case w/a long dial below a large grille **$10**

Motorola, Model 58F1, wooden tabletop model w/phonograph **$65**

Motorola, Model 58L11, portable, small high rounded rectangular mottled tan plastic case w/two large knobs, carrying handle on top, late 1950s (ILLUS., bottom of page) **$40-50**

Motorola, Model 58R11, plastic tabletop model, ca. 1947 .... **$35**

Motorola, Model 59R, Bakelite tabletop model in a simple design, ca. 1948............. **$10**

Motorola, Model 5A7, plastic portable model w/flip-up cover.. **$30**

Motorola, Model 5C1, plastic clock radio......... **$40**

Late 1950s Mottled Tan Plastic Portable Radio

Motorola Model 5X12U Ivory Plastic Radio with Large Dial

Motorola, Model 5X12U, ivory plastic case w/large round center dial w/inner perforated grille, metal stand base, two knobs, broadcast band, five tubes, AC/DC, 1950 (ILLUS., top of page)............................... **$35-45**

Motorola, Model 67F14, wooden radio & phonograph console, large.......................... **$75**

Motorola, Model 85F21, console radio w/phonograph, ca. 1948............................... **$40**

Muntz, Model R-12, plastic clock radio w/a large clock dial on the left, 1959.................. **$30**

Nordmemde, plastic tabletop model w/a large dial & large white pushbuttons, 1963.. **$85**

Nordmemde, portable plastic model w/carrying handle, 1963 .... **$30**

Northern Electric, table model, one-band, black Bakelite case w/two dials, Art Deco scrollwork, 1940s, 10 x 6 x 6 1/2" (ILLUS., bottom of page)............................. **$85**

Oceana, portable in plastic case, various colors, Japan, early 1960s........................... **$75**

Northern Electric Table Radio

Olympic Dark Brown Plastic Modernistic-style Radio

Olympic, Model 7-421W, rectangular walnut brown plastic case rounded at the right front around the round slanted dial, the left side w/horizontal wrap-around louvers, two knobs, broadcast band, five tubes, 1949 (ILLUS.)... **$70-80**

Packard Bell Model 46D Wooden Radio from 1938

Packard Bell, Model 46D, rectangular dark wood case w/metal banding around the large "Stationized" dial, AM/SW, 1938 (ILLUS.)... **$75-125**

Packard Bell Model 46H with Attractive Wooden Case

Packard Bell, Model 46H, rectangular rounded wooden case of banded veneering, "Stationized" dial, AM/short-wave, 1940 (ILLUS.) **$65-95**

Packard Bell Model 501 Rectangular Bakelite 1951 Radio

Packard Bell, Model 501, rectangular blackish brown Bakelite case w/"Stationized" dial, 1951 (ILLUS.)
.... **$35-50**

Packard Bell Model 602 Radio with Blond Wood Case

Packard Bell, Model 602, upright oblong flattened blond wood case w/long narrow dual "Stationized" dial, AM, 1952 (ILLUS., top of page)............................... **$25-50**

Panasonic, Model R-70, Panapet ball-shaped model found in a variety of bright colors, ca. 1970s... **$20**

Panasonic, Model R-72, ring-shaped case found in a variety of bright colors, 1970s **$35**

Panasonic, Model RC-57, clock radio w/fluorescent dial, ca. 1970s (ILLUS., bottom of page)... **$20**

Panasonic Model RC-57 Clock-Radio

Miniature Blue Parrot Tube Radio

Parrot, Model KS-4S1, miniature blue plastic tube radio (ILLUS.).. **$95**

Pfanstiehl Model 7 Radio

Pfanstiehl, Model 7 Overtone, "Listening to a Pfanstiehl is like being there yourself," wide wooden case w/wooden cutouts over speaker area, five-tube battery set, manufactured in Highland Park, Ill., ca. 1924, 36 x 16 x 15" (ILLUS.).. **$145**

Philco Model 10A3 Spinet-style Console

Philco, Model 10A3, console model w/attractive spinet-style cabinet, 1930s (ILLUS.) **$300**

Philco Model 18 Cathedral-style Radio

Philco, Model 18, cathedral-style wooden case w/arched lattice speaker panel above recessed dial & knobs, AM/police bands, shadow tuning meter, 1934 (ILLUS.)... **$200-250**

Philco Model 20 Cathedral-style Radio from 1930

Philco, Model 20, cathedral-style wooden case w/arched scrolling lattice speaker panel, shadow tuning meter, seven-tube, AC receiver, 1930 (ILLUS.) **$250**

Philco Model 37-602 Faux Woodgrained Case

Philco, Model 37-602, rectangular round-cornered wooden case w/faux burl woodgrained finish, streamlined speaker design, 1937 (ILLUS.) **$75-100**

Philco, Model 38-1, tall wooden floor console w/nice burl wood veneering, slanted top control panel above a tall lattice-covered cloth speaker panel, rounded front corners, AM/short-wave, 1938 (ILLUS., previous column).................................. **$100-150**

Philco, Model 39-116, nicely veneered wooden console w/large speaker below the wireless "mystery control," 1939 (ILLUS., bottom of page)..................... **$100-150**

Philco, Model 46-1201, console radio-phonograph w/a bottom drawer opening to insert records, 1946 .... **$50**

Philco Model 38-1 Tall Wooden Console

Philco Model 39-116 Wood Console with "Mystery Control"

Philco Model 46-1201 Radio-Phonograph

Philco, Model 46-1201, tabletop radio & phonograph, rounded front w/space for sliding in record, 1946 (ILLUS., top of page) **$65**

Philco, Model 46-1213, wooden console radio-phonograph w/a front door that opens for sliding out the phonograph, 1946............ **$15**

Philco, Model 48-1253, radio-phonograph in a square wooden tabletop cabinet **$20**

Philco, Model 49-1401, wood & Bakelite "boomerang" style radio-phonograph, low rectangular form w/high arched back speaker panel, 1949 (ILLUS., bottom of page)... **$75-125**

Philco, Model 49-500, Bakelite tabletop model w/a ribbed design across the front, 1949.. **$15**

Philco Model 49-1401 Radio-Phonograph in "Boomerang" Style Case

Rare Philco Model 49-501 "Boomerang" Style 1949 Bakelite Radio

Philco, Model 49-501, black Bakelite case w/"boomerang" styling, arched round speaker at one end, large dial at the other end, 1949 (ILLUS.).. **$350-500**

Classic Philco Cathedral-style Radio

Philco, Model 70, wooden Cathedral-style tabletop model, early 1930s (ILLUS.).......................... **$200-300+**

Philco Model 90 "Highboy" Floor Model Radio from 1931

Philco, Model 90, "Highboy" style floor model wooden cabinet w/a pair of tall arched doors opening to the recessed dial, knobs & lattice-covered speaker, raised on a turned trestle-style base, 1931 (ILLUS.).. **$100-125**

Philco Model 90 Cathedral-style Radio with Fine Veneering

Philco, Model 90, wooden cathedral-style tabletop model w/fine quality patterned veneering around the front, AM, 1931 (ILLUS., top of page)........................... **$350-500**

Philco, Model T-1000, plastic tabletop clock-radio, two speakers above the base, 1960 .... **$55**

Philco Jr., Model 81, wooden cathedral-style case w/a light burl wood center front framed by dark wood, AM/police band, 1933 (ILLUS., bottom of page).............. **$75-125**

Philco Jr. Model 81 Cathedral-style Radio

Radio Knight Box-form Table Radio

Radio Knight, wooden box-form tabletop model w/three large front dials, 1920s (ILLUS., top of page)................................... **$90**

Radiola, Model 20, table set w/low rectangular wood cabinet, 5-tube model, 1925 (ILLUS., bottom of page)............................. **$85**

RCA, Model 1-BT-2, tabletop plastic portable w/charger **$85**

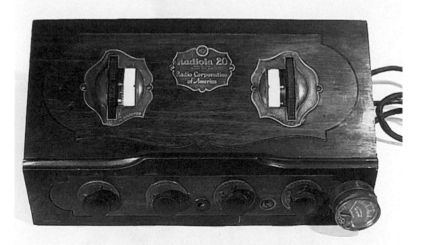

1920s Radiola Model 20 Table Style Radio

RCA Model 143 Art Deco-style Wooden Radio

RCA, Model 143, Art Deco style upright veneered wood cabinet w/a wide arched central section w/speaker grille above the dial & knobs, AM/short-wave, 1934 (ILLUS., top of page)........................... **$300-450**

RCA, Model 2R51, plastic, portable, mid-1950s **$25**

RCA, Model 54B5, portable model w/mottled brown case, the left front w/a round dial, the right front w/horizontal wraparound louvers, top carrying handle, two knobs, broadcast band, four tubes, battery-powered, 1947 (ILLUS., bottom of page)... **$35-45**

1940s RCA Portable Plastic Radio

RCA Model 65X1 Brown Plastic Table Radio

RCA, Model 65X1, dark brown plastic case, the upper front w/a curved slide rule dial, lower horizontal louvers, two knobs, broadcast band, five tubes, AC/DC, 1946 (ILLUS., top of page).............................. **$35-40**

RCA, Model 66BX, plastic portable w/aluminum trim **$65**

RCA, Model 66X1, oversized tabletop in Bakelite case, ca. 1946 (ILLUS., bottom of page)... **$45**

RCA, Model 66X11, plastic tabletop model w/Chinese-style grille, 1948 .... **$75**

RCA, Model 6HF3, nearly square simple wooden console model w/slide-out phonograph, 1956... **$25**

RCA, Model 8T10, black case w/tubular chrome frame, 1930s **$2,500**

RCA, Model 9TX-50, small wooden tabletop model, ca. 1939 .... **$40**

RCA, Model 9X571, Bakelite tabletop model w/large concentric speaker grilles, late 1940s **$45**

RCA, Model TX1J, wooden tabletop model w/dial vertically in center front, transistor chassis, 1959.. **$10**

RCA Oversized Tabletop Radio

RCA Radiola Model 111A Battery-operated 1924 Receiver

RCA, Radiola Model 111A, four-tube battery-operated receiver in wide wooden case, 1924 (ILLUS., top of page) **$175**

RCA, Radiola Model 18, wide wooden case, late 1920s... **$65**

SABA, "Sabine" model, tall glossy wooden tabletop model w/pushbuttons below the dial, ca. 1959... **$75**

Silvertone (Sears), Model 3001, plastic, 1954.. **$35**

Silvertone (Sears), Model 4569, Art Deco style wood veneered cabinet w/speakers at one end, large gold central dial, AM/short-wave, 1937 (ILLUS., bottom of page)... **$150-200**

Silvertone Model 4569 with Art Deco Wooden Case & Gold Dial

Art Deco Style Silvertone Model 6178-A Radio

Silvertone (Sears), Model 6178-A, stream-lined Art Deco style white plastic case w/a large round red dial knob at the right end, the rounded left end w/horizontal wrap-around louvers, broadcast band, five tubes, AC/DC, 1939 (ILLUS., top of page) **$130-170**

Silvertone (Sears), Model 7025, Bakelite tabletop model w/"candy cane" dial & logo design, ca. 1946 .... **$75**

Silvertone (Sears), Model 8070A, radio-phonograph in black Bakelite case, rounded end, open turntable on the top, 1948 (ILLUS., bottom of page)................ **$50-75**

Silvertone (Sears), Model 8230, larger wooden tabletop model w/simple styling w/metal & cloth grille above the dial, 1948 .... **$10**

Silvertone Model 8070A Radio-Phonograph in Bakelite Case

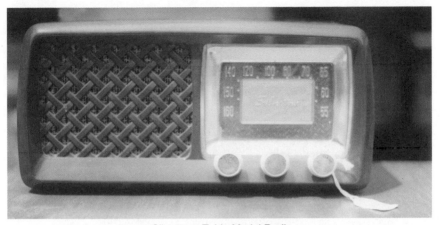

Silvertone Table Model Radio

Silvertone (Sears), plastic table model, green w/latticework on front speaker panel, 1955 (ILLUS., top of page) **$50**

Sonora, Model 100, painted Bakelite tabletop model w/wide grille slots in the front, 1946 .... **$20**

Sonora, Model WEV-262, streamlined black Bakelite case, large dial & speaker panel above four white knobs, AM/FM, 1948 (ILLUS., bottom of page)............ **$100-150**

Sparton, Model 1039, simply stylized radio-phonograph, 1940s **$45**

Sparton, Model 10BW76, console radio w/pull-out phonograph, 1940s...................... **$55**

Sparton, Model 121, simple wooden tabletop model **$30**

Sparton, Model 132, plastic oval-shaped case, ca. 1950... **$95**

Sparton, Model 301, portable w/handle on top, ca. 1950 .... **$25**

Sparton, Model 506, "Bluebird" circular blue mirror-front model **$2,500**

Sparton, Model 557, three-knob tabletop model w/blue mirror & chrome trim......... **$2,500**

Sparton, Model 5AW06, Bakelite case, mid-1940s **$35**

Speakers, some manufactured by Music Master, various sizes, name usually appears on speaker or inside the horn, price varies due to size & condition .... **$50+**

Standard, Model SR-H436, pocket-size, chrome & black case................................. **$70**

Standard, Model SR-H437, chrome & black, pocket-size **$75**

Sonora Model WEV-262 Bakelite AM/FM Radio from 1948

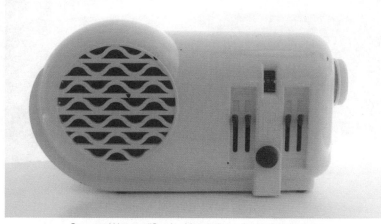

Stewart Warner "Senior Varsity" Art Deco Style Radio

Stewart Warner Model 62T36 Catalin Radio

Stewart Warner, Model 07-58 "Senior Varsity," Art Deco style white plastic case w/a small dial at the right front, the left rounded end w/a round grille composed of wavy cutouts, two knobs, broadcast band, five tubes, AC/DC, 1939 (ILLUS., top of page) **$220-280**

Stewart Warner, Model 62T36, mottled brown Catalin w/dark yellow grille & knobs, 1946 (ILLUS., middle from top) **$500-600**

Stewart Warner, Model A51, tall narrow brown or painted Bakelite tabletop model, two knobs & dial at the top, 1946 .... **$75**

Stewart Warner Model A51T4 Oblong Black Bakelite Radio from 1947

Stewart Warner, Model A51T4, upright oblong black Bakelite case w/large round dials at the top ends, dial & speaker in the center, 1947 (ILLUS.) **$75-100**

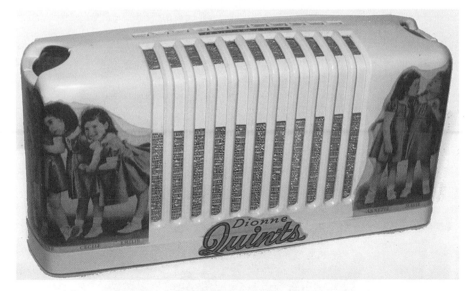

Dionne Quints Novelty Radio

Stewart Warner, Model A6S, Dionne Quints novelty radio (ILLUS.) **$750**

Stewart Warner Model R-1803 Chair-side Model with Open Shelves

Stewart Warner, Model R-1803, wooden floor chair-side style, upright rectangular cabinet w/open shelves at the back half, AM/short-wave, 1937 (ILLUS., top of page) **$75-100**

Stewart Warner Model R1866 "Tombstone" Style 1937 Radio

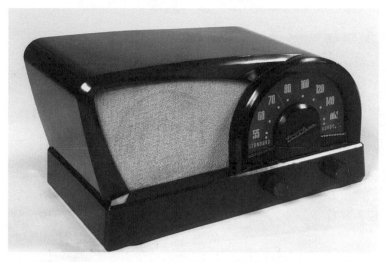

Truetone Model -D-2017 Bakelite "Boomerang" Style Radio from 1951

Stewart Warner, Model R1866, upright wooden "tombstone" style case w/lattice-covered grille above the round dial & small knobs, AM/short-wave, 1937 (ILLUS., bottom previous page) **$200-250**

Stromberg Carlson, Model 180, floor model w/cabinet doors & acoustical sound system, 1936... **$300**

Sylvania, Model 2301, "Star Timer," stylish clock radio, late 1950s **$65**

Sylvania, Model 2302, "Night Lighter," stylish clock radio, late 1950s........................... **$65**

Sylvania, Model 5151, "Nocturne," plastic tabletop model w/knob on side, 1957........... **$35**

Toshiba, Model 6TP-385, transistor-type radio w/chrome grille................................... **$40**

Truetone, Model D-2017, dark blackish brown "boomerang" style Bakelite case, high pointed & rounded speaker panel at one end opposite the large arched dial, 1951 (ILLUS., top of page)................. **$125-175**

Truetone, Model D-2610, brown plastic case w/a large central front square dial, the right & left ends composed of horizontal louvers, two knobs, broadcast band, five tubes, AC/DC, 1946 (ILLUS., bottom of page)..................................... **$75-90**

Truetone Model D-2610 Plastic Radio from 1946

Truetone Model D-727 Radio with Pushbutton Tuning

Truetone, Model D-2613, painted Bakelite tabletop model w/three knobs at the bottom front & dial near the top, 1946............... **$20**

Truetone, Model D-2616, painted Bakelite tabletop model w/a curved front, 1946......... **$45**

Truetone, Model D-3809, plastic portable model w/carrying handle on top, 1946......... **$10**

Truetone, Model D-727, rectangular veneered wood cabinet w/black top & bottom banding, motorized pushbutton tuning, AM/short-wave, 1938 (ILLUS., top of page).. **$200-250**

U.S. Apex, Model 8A, stepped arched "tombstone" style wood-veneered case w/ornate lattice over the top speaker panel, 1931 (ILLUS., bottom of page)....... **$250-350**

Victor Talking Machine, Model 143, table model w/illuminated dial, four bands & four controls, 1930s, 13 x 16 x 20" **$150**

Early U.S. Apex Model 8A "Tombstone" Style Radio from 1931

Westinghouse Model 667A Canadian Radio

Westinghouse, Model 667A, veneered wood case w/wrap-around speakers at each end, AM/short-wave, Canada, 1936 (ILLUS., top of page)............................ **$75-100**

Westinghouse, Model H-126, "Little Jewel," refrigerator-shaped tall painted Bakelite model w/brass center section & swing-up handle **$75**

Westinghouse 1948 Radio-Phonograph

Westinghouse Five-band Radio

Westinghouse, Model H-171, blond wood upright chair-side style radio-phonograph w/removable radio, cabinet door in the base, 1948 (ILLUS., bottom previous page) **$50-75**

Westinghouse, Model H-327, large plastic tabletop model w/plastic bar-patterned grille, ca. 1950 .... **$10**

Westinghouse, oversized brown wood table model, five-band, w/speakers at bottom & four large dials & six small dials, 1940s, 20 x 11 x 16" (ILLUS., top of page) **$100**

Zenith, Model 10-S-464, wooden tall floor console, a stepped top above the black round dial, the lower cabinet w/horizontal bars over the cloth-covered speaker, pushbuttons, one knob, broadcast band, 10-tube, AC/short-wave, 1940 (ILLUS.) **$300-400**

Zenith 1935 Wooden "Tombstone" Radio

Zenith, Model 5-S-29, wooden tabletop "tombstone" style case, round black dial in lower front, upper w/cloth-covered grille w/cut-outs, four knobs, broadcast band, short-wave, five-tube, 1935 (ILLUS.) **$150-180**

Zenith Model 10-S-464 Floor Console

Streamlined Art Deco Zenith Model 5R-312 Radio

Zenith, Model 5D011, square wooden tabletop model, mid-1940s.............................. **$25**

Zenith, Model 5R-312, dark brown plastic case, the rectangular right end enclosing the rectangular dial, the wide rounded left end composed of raised horizontal wraparound louvers, pushbutton controls, two knobs, broadcast band, five tubes, AC, 1938 (ILLUS., top of page).................. **$110-140**

Zenith, Model 6-D-410, small brown Bakelite case, dial on the right front, vertical wrap-over grille on the left, one tuning & one thumbwheel knob, broadcast band, six-tube including ballast, AC/DC, 1939 (ILLUS., bottom of page)................ **$70-80**

Zenith, Model 6D311, Wavemagnet Bakelite tabletop model, late 1930s........... **$175**

Zenith, Model 6G001, Trans-Oceanic model in cloth-covered case, mid-1940s, average condition **$95**

Zenith, Model 7H820, large plastic tabletop model, three-band, ca. 1949 .... **$45**

Small Zenith Model 6-D-410 Bakelite Radio

1949 Zenith "Transoceanic" Radio in Wood Cabinet

Zenith, Model 8G005 - &TZ1, "Transoceanic" model in black wood cabinet w/carrying handle, AM/short-wave, 1949 (ILLUS., top of page) **$75-100**

Zenith, Model 8H023, plastic, tabletop, three-band, mid-1940s **$55**

Zenith, Model H725, Bakelite tabletop model w/handle, 1950 .... **$35**

Zenith, Model J664, low squared black Bakelite radio-phonograph w/large round dial at the front & hinged cover, 1953 (ILLUS., bottom of page) **$100-150**

Zenith Model J664 Bakelite Radio-Phonograph

Deep Pink Zenith Model R512V Radio from 1955

Zenith, Model R512V, deep pink long plastic case, the right front w/a half-round dial, the center w/a checkered grille w/crest, raised on outswept feet, two knobs, six pushbuttons on top, broadcast band, AC/DC, 1955 (ILLUS., top of page) **$60-70**

Zenith, Royal Model 755, leatherette-covered portable model **$30**

Zvezda, Model 54 "Red Star," streamlined mottled red cabinet w/metal bands across the front & large central mirror dial, AM/short-wave, Russia, 1954 (ILLUS., bottom of page).................... **$350-500**

Russian Zvezda Model 54 Radio with Metal Cabinet

Transistors

Admiral, Model 581, simple plastic
design, ca. 1959.. $10

Admiral, Model 7L12, large portable transistor w/a solar attachment (ILLUS., middle of page) $250

Arvin, Model 62R49, tall leather & metal
case, 1960 .... $10

Boy's Radio, Model NR-23, red & white case, two-transistor pocket-type, w/box, 1950s (ILLUS., bottom of page)................. $25

Channel Master, "Maverick" model, large plastic battery-operated tabletop radio, ca. 1959... $10

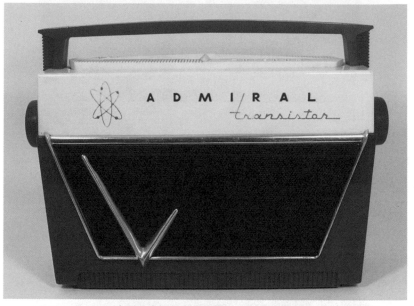

Large Admiral Model 7L12 Transistor

1950s Boy's Transistor Pocket Radio

Common Channel Master Model 6506 Transistor Radio

Channel Master, Model 6506, long six-transistor radio, common, late 1950s (ILLUS.) **$20**

Coronet Boy's Radio Transistor

Coronet, Boy's Radio, two-transistor model (ILLUS.) **$20**

Emerson "Miracle Wand" Transistor

DuMont, Model RA-354, leather portable model w/top carrying handle, ca. 1956 .... **$15**

DuMont, Model RA-902, leather portable model w/top carrying handle, ca. 1956 .... **$15**

Emerson, "Miracle Wand" style large portable transistor w/large top handle (ILLUS., top of page).. **$35**

Emerson, Model 555, "The All-American," long blue case w/gold grille front, 1950s (ILLUS., bottom of page)............................ **$45**

Emerson Model 555 "All-American" Transistor

Red Emerson Satellite Transistor

Emerson, Satellite model, red case, unusual variation of the Model 888 (ILLUS.).................................... **$95**

GE Model 678 Early Transistor Radio

General Electric, Model 678, rectangular blue plastic case w/delicate grillework, GE's first transistor radio
(ILLUS.).. **$70**

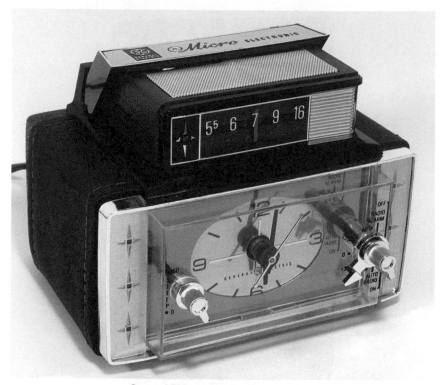

General Electric Piggyback Radio/Clock

General Electric, Model C-2450, piggyback style transistor radio on clock, 1970s (ILLUS.) **$65**

General Electric Model P674 Tabletop Transistor

General Electric, Model P674, oversized four-tube tabletop transistor, AC/DC power (ILLUS.) **$10**

General Electric Model P715 Transistor with Case & Accessories

General Electric, Model P715, w/case & accessories, late 1950s (ILLUS.)... **$25**

Common General Electric Model P807 Transistor

General Electric, Model P807 or P808, black plastic portable model w/gold grille at the left & large round dial at the right, common, each (ILLUS.) **$10**

GE Model P850 Radio in Chrome & Black

General Electric, Model P850, chrome & black case w/oversized key ring handle (ILLUS.) **$15**

Global 9 Red Transistor Radio

Global 9, Model GR-900, red case (ILLUS.) **$85**

Heathkit Model XR-1 Kit Transistor

Heathkit, Model XR-1, transistor assembled from a kit (ILLUS.) **$35**

Black & Gold Hitachi Model TH-666

Hitachi, Model TH-666, black & gold case (ILLUS.) **$65**

Imperial AM/FM Transistor Radio

Imperial, AM/FM transistor in maroon case, made in Hong Kong, 1960s (ILLUS.) **$10**

Lloyd's Model 8 Super Micro Radio

Lloyd's, Model 8, Super Micro transistor radio (ILLUS.)... **$45**

Magnavox Model AM-60 Transistor

Magnavox, Model AM-60, 1960s model
transistor (ILLUS., top of page)................... **$10**
Philco, Model T-54, "The Valley Forge,"
large plastic & leather portable
model, ca. 1960... **$10**

Philco, Model T-7, long black & white case,
late 1950s, Philco's first transistor
(ILLUS., bottom of page)............................. **$75**

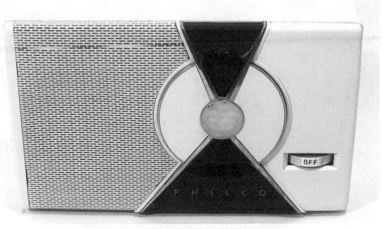

Philco Model T-7, Philco's First Transistor

Raytheon Model 8TP Early Transistor

Raytheon, Model 8TP, early large leather-covered transistor radio, overhead handle (ILLUS.) **$125**

Early Raytheon Model T-100 Transistor

Raytheon, Model T-100, early transistor radio (ILLUS.) **$200**

Regency Model TR-1 - The First Transistor

Regency, Model TR-1, black plastic case, the first transistor radio (ILLUS.)... **$185**

Regency Model TR-5B Leather-cased Transistor

Regency, Model TR-5B, leather-cased transistor (ILLUS.).. **$35**

Unusual Regency Model TR-6 in Black Leather Case

Regency, Model TR-6, large black leather-covered portable model, unusual (ILLUS., top of page)................................... $55

Regency, Model XR-2A, miniature two-transistor model w/earphone (ILLUS., bottom of page).. $125

Sony, Model 2F-23W, small transistor AM/FM model, late 1950s........................... $10

Regency XR-2A Mini Radio with Earphone

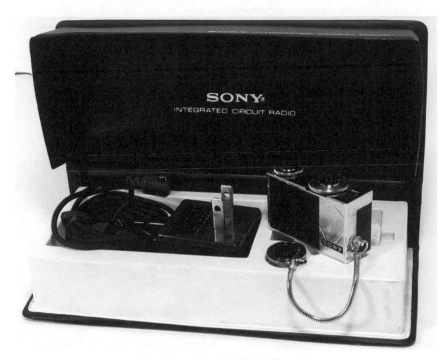

Small Sony Model IRC-120 Transistor

Sony, Model IRC-120, black & chrome 1 1/4" integrated circuit radio (ILLUS., top of page) **$145**

Sony, Model TR-1819, cube-shaped plastic & metal, 1960s, common **$10**

Sony, Model TR-624, desktop style black plastic & metal transistor radio (ILLUS., bottom of page).. **$25**

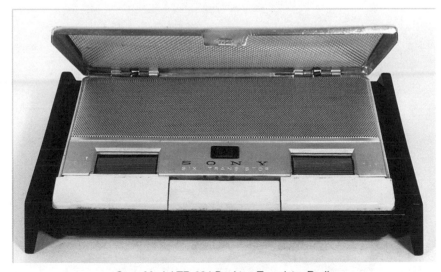

Sony Model TR-624 Desktop Transistor Radio

Brown Standard Micronic Ruby Radio

Standard, Micronic Ruby Model SR-436,
   brown & silver case, in original box
   (ILLUS., top of page)................................... **$40**

Standard, Micronic Ruby Model SR-G430,
   tiny red & silver case, in original box
   (ILLUS., bottom of page)............................. **$70**

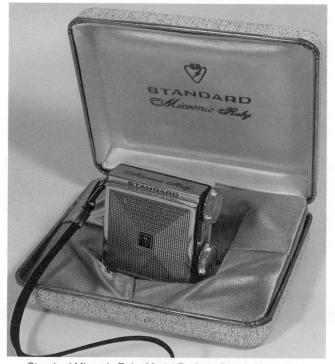

Standard Micronic Ruby Model Radio in Red & Silver Case

Sylvania Model 4P19WD Large Coat Pocket Sized Transistor

Sylvania, Model 4P19WD, white plastic case, large coat pocket size, 1960s (ILLUS.)............................ **$15**

Unusual Sylvania Thunderbird Model

Sylvania, Thunderbird model w/unusual flip-up design (ILLUS.) **$150**

Toshiba Model 10TL-429F AM/FM Model

Toshiba, Model 10TL-429F, AM/FM model (ILLUS.)... **$25**

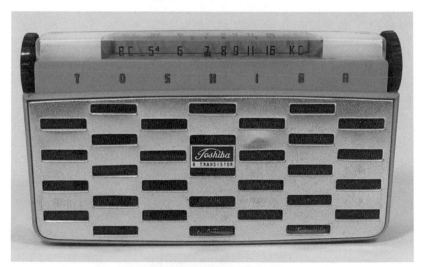

Toshiba Model 8TM-294 Transistor

Toshiba, Model 8TM-294, wide case in blue & white (ILLUS.) **$50**

Toshiba Model TR-193 "Lace" Radio

Toshiba, Model TR-193 "Lace" design model, mint condition (ILLUS.) **$200**

Truetone Red Super Six Transistor

Truetone, Super 6 Model DC2902, tall red plastic portable transistor (ILLUS.).. **$55**

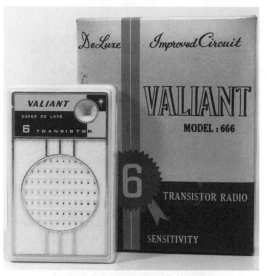

Valiant Super DeLuxe Model 666

Valiant, Super DeLuxe Model 666, made in Hong Kong, 1970s (ILLUS.) **$10**

Early Zenith Model 500 Transistor

Zenith, Model 500, early transistor w/hand-wired chassis (ILLUS.) **$175**

Zenith Model 500H Early Transistor

Zenith, Model 500H, 1962-63 (ILLUS.) **$125-150**

Zenith Royal 16 Billfold-style Radio

Zenith, Royal 16 model, billfold-style case (ILLUS.) **$25**

Zenith Royal 555 Solar Radio Kit

Zenith, Royal 555 model, working solar radio, complete kit (ILLUS.)........................... **$175**

Microphones

Early E.V. Ring Mike from the 1920s

E.V., ring-style microphone on short pedestal base, 1929 (ILLUS.)... **$250-350**

RCA Model 77DX Microphone

RCA, Model 77DX, long oblong head fitted w/NBC broadcasting sign, on adjustable stand, 1952 (ILLUS., top of page) **$1,200-2,500**

Shure, Model 55, oblong grooved head on adjustable standard w/domed base, 1957 (ILLUS., bottom of page)............ **$100-175**

Shure Model 55 1950s Microphone

PART 2

Televisions

The most important factors in the value of early sets are rarity and cosmetic condition. Relatively few black and white sets were made before 1950, and few color sets were made before 1960. Therefore, these sets are the most desired by collectors and sets manufactured after these years, with a few exceptions, have almost no value. Table model sets are preferred, since they occupy less space and cost less to ship. Console sets can cost up to $500 to ship, often much more than their value. This guide lists only sets that are in demand by collectors.

Generally, the value of a set is not affected by whether or not it is in working condition. Even if an old set is working, it won't be reliable unless it is restored by a competent technician, and many collectors do their own restoration. Sets that have been restored usually bring a higher price than unrestored sets. Cosmetic condition is very important; a set in mint condition will bring twice the price or more than one in fair condition. It is also important that the set be complete with all its knobs and its back.

Because of the limited number of collectors, prices very greatly for the same model set. For this guide, eBay prices are assumed since this is the predominant way early sets are now marketed. Often lower prices will be seen at flea markets and swap meets.

Note: The inch size of the screen is noted at the end of each listing.

Admiral, Ambassador color console model, 1957, 21" (ILLUS., bottom of page) **$400**
Admiral, Model 12X12, wooden tabletop, 1950, 12" screen... **$50**
Admiral, Model 14R12, Bakelite tabletop, 1950, 14".. **$75**

Admiral Ambassador Early Color Set

Admiral Model 14YP3 Metal Portable TV

Admiral, Model 14YP3/T015AL, portable model in a green metal cabinet, top handle, 1956, 14" (ILLUS., top of page)........ **$50-75**

Admiral, Model 16R12, Bakelite console, 1950, 16".. **$40**

Admiral, Model 17T11, Bakelite tabletop w/"Chinese" grille, 1948, 7" **$300**

Admiral, Model 17T12, Bakelite tabletop w/checkerboard grille, 1948, 7"................. **$150**

Admiral, Model 19A11, Bakelite tabletop w/checkerboard grille, 1948, 7" (ILLUS., bottom of page).. **$150**

Admiral Model 19A11 Tabletop Set

Admiral Tabletop Model from 1948

Admiral, Model 19A11, tabletop model in a blond wood cabinet, 1948, 7" (ILLUS., top of page).. **$75-125**

Admiral, Model 19A12, Bakelite tabletop w/"Chinese" grille, 1948, 7" **$300**

Admiral, Model 19T1, Bakelite tabletop model, 1948, 7" **$150**

Admiral, Model 20A1, wooden tabletop, 1949, 10".. **$75**

Admiral, Model 20B1, wooden tabletop, 1949, 12" **$75**

Admiral, Model 20T1, Bakelite console model, 1950, 14".. **$75**

Admiral, Model 20X11, Bakelite tabletop model, 1950, 10" (ILLUS., bottom of page)... **$100**

Admiral, Model 20X112, Bakelite console model, 1950, 10".................................... **$100**

Admiral, Model 20X12, Bakelite console model, 1948, 10".................................... **$400**

Admiral, Model 20X122, Bakelite console model, 1950, 10".. **$400**

Admiral Model 20X11 Bakelite Tabletop Television from 1950

Admiral Model 20X136 Table Model

Admiral, Model 20X136, wooden tabletop, 1949, 12" (ILLUS., top of page) **$150**

Admiral, Model 20Y1, wooden tabletop, 1949, 10" **$75**

Admiral, Model 24A12, Bakelite console model, 1948, 12" **$200**

Admiral, Model 24R12, Bakelite console model, 1950, 14" **$50**

Admiral, Model 2OUB6CB, console model in a wooden cabinet swiveling on a base composed of four pointed legs, 1950s (ILLUS., bottom of page)............................ **$70**

Admiral, Model 30A1, wooden console model, 1949, 10" **$100**

1950s Swiveling Admiral Console TV

Airline Model 84HA-3002 Tabletop Set

Admiral, Model C223A, wooden console model raised on four pointed legs, knobs at the top front, ca. 1956, 21".......................... **$75**

Admiral, Model C2516, wooden console model w/simple styling, 1954, 24"............... **$45**

Admiral, Model T23B, tabletop model w/a wood-grained metal cabinet raised on large removable legs, 1956, 21" **$55**

Air King, Model 12C1, wooden tabletop, 1949, 12".. **$50**

Air King, Model 16C1, wooden console model, 1950, 16" **$50**

Air King, Model A-1000, wooden tabletop, 1948, 10".. **$200**

Air King, Model A-1001, wooden tabletop, 1949, 10".. **$175**

Air King, Model A-1001A, wooden console model, 1949, 10" **$75**

Air King, Model A-1016, wooden console model, 1949, 16" **$75**

Air King, Model A-2000, wooden tabletop, 1949, 10".. **$150**

Air King, Model A-2002, wooden console model, 1949, 10".. **$75**

Air King, Model A-711, wooden tabletop, 1950, 12".. **$50**

Air King, Model A-712, wooden tabletop, 1950, 12".. **$50**

Airline, Model 05GSE-3020, wooden tabletop, 1950, 12".. **$50**

Airline, Model 84GSE-3010, wooden projection console model, 1948 .... **$100**

Airline, Model 84GSE-3011, cloth-covered portable model, 1949, 7" **$250**

Airline, Model 84HA-3002, wooden tabletop w/13-channel pushbutton tuning, 1948, 7" (ILLUS., top of page) **$350**

Airline, Model 94BR-3004, wooden tabletop, 1949, 10".. **$150**

Airline, Model 94BR-3005, wooden console model, 1949, 10".. **$75**

Airline, Model 94BR-3017, wooden tabletop, 1948, 7".. **$125**

Airline, Model 94GSE-3015, leatherette tabletop w/"telephoto control," 1948, 7" **$300**

Airline Model 94GSE with Radio & Phonograph

Ambassador Model 612A Console

Airline, Model 94GSE-3018, wooden table-top w/45 rpm turntable & radio, 1948, 7" (ILLUS., bottom previous page) **$400**

Airline, Model 94GSE-3025, wooden table-top, 1949, 16" **$125**

Airline, Model 94GSE-3033, wooden console model, 1949, 16" **$75**

Airline, Model 94WG-3006, blond wood console model, 1949, 10" **$75**

Airline, Model 94WG-3009, wooden console model, 1949, 10" **$75**

Airline, Model 94WG-3022, wooden table-top, 1949, 12" **$150**

Airline, Model 94WG-3029, blond wood console model, 1949, 12" **$100**

Ambassador, Model 612A, wooden console model, 1949, 12" (ILLUS., top of page) **$100**

Rare Early Andrea Model 1-F-5

Extremely Rare Early Andrea Console Model with Mirror in Lid & Radio

AMC (Aimcee), Model 116T, wooden table-
top, 1951, 16".. **$75**
AMC (Aimcee), Model 120C, wooden table-
top, 1950, 12".. **$125**

Andrea, Model 1-F-5, tabletop model, 1939,
5" (ILLUS., bottom of previous page)
.... **$8,000**
Andrea, Model 2-F-12, console w/mirror in
lid w/radio, 1939, 12" (ILLUS., top of
page).. **$12,000**

Rare 1939 Andrea Model 8-F-12 Console

Andrea, Model 8-F-12, console w/mirror in lid w/radio & phonograph, 1939, 12" (ILLUS., top of page)............................ **$15,000**

Andrea, Model CO-VJ12, wooden console model w/radio & phonograph, 1948, 12" **$125-150**

Andrea, Model CO-VK15, wooden console model w/radio & phonograph, 1948, 15" **$125-150**

Andrea, Model CVL-16, wooden console model, 1951, 16"... **$50**

Early Andrea Model KTE-5 Kit TV in Original Cabinet

Andrea, Model KTE-5, kit TV in original wood cabinet, 1938, 5" (ILLUS.)... **$3,500**

Andrea Model KTE-5 with No Cabinet

Andrea, Model KTE-5, kit TV, no cabinet, 1939, 5" (ILLUS.).. **$6,000**

Andrea Model T-VJ12 TV with Radio

Andrea, Model T-VJ12, wooden tabletop w/radio, 1947, 12" (ILLUS.) **$500**

Andrea Model T-VK12 Wooden Tabletop

Andrea, Model T-VK12, wooden tabletop w/radio, 1948, 12" (ILLUS.) **$300**

Arvin Model 4080T Metal Portable

Artone, Model AR-23-TV, wooden tabletop, 1948, 10"... **$300**

Arvin, Model 2120C, wooden console model, 1949, 12".. **$125**

Arvin, Model 2121TM, wooden tabletop model, 1949, 12"..................................... **$125**

Arvin, Model 2122TM, wooden tabletop model, 1949, 12"..................................... **$125**

Arvin, Model 2123TM, wooden tabletop model, 1949, 12"....................................... **$75**

Arvin, Model 2124CCM, wooden console w/radio & phonograph model, 1949, 12"...... **$75**

Arvin, Model 2126CM, wooden console model, 1949, 12"..................................... **$100**

Arvin, Model 2161TM, wooden tabletop, 1949, 16".. **$125**

Arvin, Model 2164CM, wooden console model w/radio & phonograph, 1949, 16"
.... **$75**

Arvin, Model 3100TB, blond wood tabletop model, 1949, 10"...................................... **$175**

Arvin, Model 3100TM, wooden tabletop, 1949, 10"... **$175**

Arvin, Model 3101CM, wooden console model, 1949, 10"..................................... **$125**

Arvin, Model 3120C, wooden console model, 1949, 12".. **$125**

Arvin, Model 3121TM, wooden tabletop, 1949, 12"... **$150**

Arvin, Model 3160CM, wooden console model, 1949, 16"..................................... **$200**

Arvin, Model 4080T, metal portable model, 1950, 8" (ILLUS., top of page) **$175**

Arvin, Model 5204CM, wooden console model, 1950, 20".. **$50**

Arvin, Model 5206C, wooden console model, 1950, 20"... **$50**

Arvin, Model AR-23-TV, wooden tabletop, 1948, 10"... **$250**

Atwater, wooden tabletop model, 1949, 12"
.... **$325**

Automatic, Model TV-1049, wooden tabletop, 1949, 10".. **$150**

Automatic, Model TV-1050, wooden console model, 1949, 10" **$100**

Automatic, Model TV-1055, wooden console model, 1949, 10" **$100**

Automatic, Model TV-1249, wooden tabletop, 1949, 12".. **$150**

Automatic, Model TV-1250, wooden console model, 1949, 12" **$150**

Automatic, Model TV-1649, wooden tabletop, 1949, 16".. **$125**

Automatic, Model TV-1650, wooden console model, 1949, 16" **$100**

Automatic, Model TV-707, blond wood tabletop, 1948, 7".................................. **$400-600**

Automatic Model TV-709 Tabletop Set

Automatic, Model TV-709, wooden table-top, 1948, 7" (ILLUS., top of page) **$500**

Automatic, Model TV-710, wooden console model, 1947, 7" **$1,500**

Automatic, Model TV-P490, cloth-covered portable w/built-in magnifier, 1948, 7"..... **$1,200**

Baird, British "Townsman" console model, wooden cabinet, 1949, 12" (ILLUS., bottom of page).. **$500**

British "Townsman" Console Television

Baird Model 165 "Everyman" Set

Baird, Model 165, British "Everyman" set, 1949, 9" (ILLUS.)... **$250**

British Baird Model T-163

Baird, Model T-163, British "Portable" set, 1948, 9" (ILLUS.) **$300**

Extremely Rare Early Baird British Televisor

Baird, Televisor model, British mechanical set w/metal cabinet, 1930 (ILLUS., top of page) **$18,000**

Belmont-Raytheon, Model 16DX21, wooden console "Observer" model, 1948, 10" **$500**

Belmont-Raytheon, Model 21A21, wooden tabletop w/slide rule dial, 1946, 7" (ILLUS., bottom of page) **$600**

Belmont-Raytheon, Model 7DX21, wooden tabletop, 1948, 7" **$400**

Belmont-Raytheon, Model 7DX22-P, leatherette-covered portable, 1948, 7" **$250**

Belmont-Raytheon Model 21A21

Belmont-Raytheon Model C1104 Porthole Console Model

Belmont-Raytheon, Model C1104, porthole wooden console model, 1950, 12" (ILLUS.)....................... **$150**

Belmont-Raytheon Model M1101 Porthole Tabletop Model

Belmont-Raytheon, Model M1101, porthole wooden tabletop, 1950, 12" (ILLUS.)................................ **$300**

Belmont-Raytheon Wooden Porthole Tabletop TV

Belmont-Raytheon, Model M1106, porthole wooden tabletop, 1950, 12" (ILLUS.,
top of page) **$300**
Belmont-Raytheon, Model M1601, port-
hole wooden console model, 1950, 16" **$200**
Bendix, Model 2001, wooden tabletop,
1950, 10" **$200**

Bendix, Model 2020, wooden tabletop,
1949, 12" (ILLUS., bottom of page) **$125**
Bendix, Model 2025, wooden tabletop,
1950, 12" **$100**
Bendix, Model 2051, wooden tabletop,
1950, 16" **$100**

Bendix Model 2020 Tabletop TV Set

Bendix Model 235-MIU Tabletop Set

Bendix, Model 235-MIU, wooden tabletop w/push-button tuning, 1949, 10" (ILLUS., top of page) **$200**

Bendix, Model 3001, wooden console model, 1950, 10" **$75**

Bendix, Model 3030, wooden console model, 1950, 10" **$75**

Bendix, Model 3033, wooden console model, 1950, 12" **$75**

Bendix, Model 3051, wooden console model, 1950, 16" **$75**

Bendix, Model 325M8, wooden console model w/radio & phonograph, 1949, 10" **$75**

Bendix, Model 6001, wooden console model w/double doors, 1950, 16" **$75**

Bendix, Model 6002, wooden console model, 1950, 16" **$75**

Bendix, Model 6003, wooden console model, 1950, 16" **$75**

Bendix, Model 6100, wooden console model w/radio & phonograph, 1950, 16" **$75**

Bush, Model TV-12, British Bakelite-cased tabletop model, 1949, 9" (ILLUS., bottom of page) **$800**

Bush, Model TV-22, British Bakelite-cased tabletop, 1950, 12" **$500**

British Bush Model TV-12 Table Model

Capehart-Farnsworth Model 610-P TV

Bush, Model TV-62, British Bakelite-cased tabletop, 1956, 9".................................... **$400**

Capehart-Farnsworth, Model 15C215, "Neptune," simple wooden console model, 1955 .... **$25**

Capehart-Farnsworth, Model 16T245, Moderne-style large tabletop cabinet on four bent-wire legs, 1953, 24" **$95**

Capehart-Farnsworth, Model 3001, wooden tabletop, 1950, 12" **$200**

Capehart-Farnsworth, Model 321M, wooden tabletop, 1950, 16" **$175**

Capehart-Farnsworth, Model 325F, wooden console model w/double doors, 1950, 16"... **$75**

Capehart-Farnsworth, Model 4001, wooden console w/radio & phonograph, 1950, 12"... **$75**

Capehart-Farnsworth, Model 501-P, blond wood console model, 1948, 10"................ **$300**

Capehart-Farnsworth, Model 610-P, wooden tabletop model, 1947, 10" (ILLUS., top of page)................................ **$600**

Capehart-Farnsworth, Model 651-P, wooden tabletop, 1947, 10" **$600**

Capehart-Farnsworth, Model 661-P, tall console model, 1947, 10" (ILLUS., below) **$500**

Capehart-Farnsworth Tall Console Set

Rare Capehart-Farnsworth Color Console

Capehart-Farnsworth, Model CXC-12, color console model, 1954, 19" (ILLUS.) **$5,000**
Capehart-Farnsworth, Model GV-260, tabletop, 1947, 10" **$500**

Capehart-Farnsworth, Model U-12-A, wooden tabletop, 1949, 10" **$200**

Small Casio Model TV-30S

Casio, Model TV-30S, small LCD, 1986, 2 1/2" (ILLUS., top of page) **$50**

CBS Columbia, Model 10FM, wooden tabletop w/FM radio, 1948, 10" **$600**

CBS Columbia, Model 10TV, wooden tabletop, 1948, 10" **$600**

CBS Columbia, Model 12CC2, experimental color-drum set, 1951 .... **$10,000**

CBS Columbia, Model 12FM, wooden tabletop w/FM radio, 1948, 12" **$500**

CBS Columbia, Model 12TV, wooden tabletop, 1948, 12" **$500**

CBS Columbia, Model 205C1, color console model w/round screen, 1955, 19".... **$4,000**

CBS Columbia, Model 20C, wooden console model, 1950, 20" **$50**

CBS Columbia, Model 20M, metal-cased tabletop, 1950, 20" **$75**

CBS Columbia, Model 20T, wooden tabletop, 1950, 20" **$75**

CBS Columbia, Model 22C05, wooden console model, 1955, 21" **$50**

CBS Columbia, Model RX-90, color console set, 1954, 15" (ILLUS., bottom of page).. **$5,000**

Certified Radio Laboratories, Model 47-71, TV kit w/no cabinet, 1947, 7" **$600**

CBS Columbia Model RX-90 Early Color Console

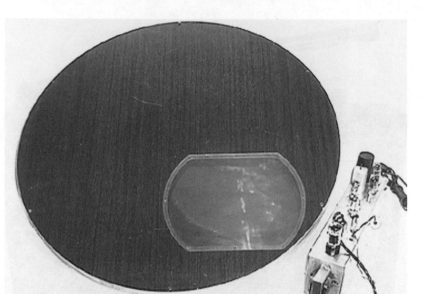

Unusual Col-R-Tel TV Attachment

Certified Radio Laboratories, Model 48-10, TV kit, no cabinet, 1948, 10" **$550**

Certified Radio Laboratories, Model 49-10, TV kit, no cabinet, 1949, 10" **$500**

Cleerview, Hollywood model, blond wood console model w/pivot screen, 1947, 15" **$1,500**

Cleerview, Regency model, wooden console model w/double doors, 1947, 15" **$1,000**

Col-R-Tel, color wheel attachment, produces a color image on a black & white TV, 1956 (ILLUS., top of page) **$750-1,800**

Coronado, console model w/RCA 721 chassis, 1948, 10" **$250**

Coronado, Model 94TV2-43-8970, wooden console model, 1949, 10" **$100**

Coronado, Model 94TV2-43-8973, wooden console model, 1949, 12" **$100**

Coronado, Model 94TV2-43-8985, wooden tabletop, 1949, 10" **$150**

Coronado, Model 94TV2-43-8987, wooden tabletop, 1949, 12" **$150**

Coronado, Model FA-438965, wooden tabletop, 1949, 7" **$350**

Coronado, Model TV43-8960, wooden tabletop, 1949, 10" **$150**

Cromwell, wooden tabletop, 1949, 10" **$250**

Crosley Model 10-401 Table Model

Crosley Model 348-CP Swing-a-View Set

Crosley, Model 10-401, Bakelite-cased tabletop, 1950, 10" (ILLUS., bottom previous page) **$175**

Crosley, Model 10-428, Bakelite-cased tabletop, 1950, 12" **$100**

Crosley, Model 10-428, wooden tabletop, 1950, 14" **$75**

Crosley, Model 10-429, wooden console model, 1950, 16" **$50**

Crosley, Model 11-443, wooden console model, 1950, 19" **$50**

Crosley, Model 11-465, wooden tabletop, 1950, 16" **$75**

Crosley, Model 307-TA, wooden tabletop model, 1948, 10" **$200**

Crosley, Model 348-CP, Swing-a-View console model w/swiveling tube, 1946, 10" (ILLUS., top of page) **$600**

Crosley, Model 9-403M, wooden tabletop model w/continuous tuner, 1949, 10" (ILLUS., bottom of page) **$150**

Crosley Model 9-403M Tabletop TV Set

Crosley Model 9-425 Leatherette Suitcase-style Television

Crosley, Model 9-407, wooden tabletop model w/continuous tuner, 1949, 12"......... **$125**

Crosley, Model 9-409M, wooden console model w/double doors, 1949, 12".............. **$100**

Crosley, Model 9-414, wooden console model w/double doors, 1949, 10".............. **$100**

Crosley, Model 9-419M, wooden tabletop, 1949, 12".. **$125**

Crosley, Model 9-420M, wooden console model, 1949, 12" **$100**

Crosley, Model 9-422M, wooden console model, 1949, 10" **$100**

Crosley, Model 9-423M, wooden console model w/double doors & radio & phonograph, 1949, 16".. **$100**

Crosley, Model 9-424B, blond wood console model, 1949, 10" **$125**

Crosley, Model 9-425, leatherette suitcase-style, 1948, 7" (ILLUS., top of page) **$200**

Crosley, Model AT10B, large tabletop model w/a blond wood-finished metal cabinet, ca. 1965.. **$25**

Crosley, Model DC18N, wooden console w/Provincial styling, 1965, 21" **$25**

Crosley, Model EU-30, wooden console model w/DuMont chassis, 1951, 30"....... **$1,000**

Dewald, Model BT-100, wooden tabletop, 1948, 10"... **$300**

Dewald, Model CT-101, wooden console model, 1949, 16"..................................... **$100**

Dewald, Model CT-102, wooden tabletop, 1949, 10"... **$300**

Dewald, Model CT-103, wooden console model, 1949, 10"..................................... **$150**

Dewald, Model CT-104, wooden tabletop, 1949, 10"... **$300**

Dewald, Model DT-102, wooden tabletop, 1949, 10"... **$300**

Dewald, Model DT-120, wooden tabletop, 1949, 12"... **$250**

Dewald, Model DT-160, wooden tabletop, 1950, 16"... **$125**

Dewald, Model DT-190, wooden tabletop, 1950, 19"... **$125**

Dewald, Model ET-140, wooden tabletop, 1950, 14"... **$100**

DuMont, Model 180, pre-war wooden console model w/four-channel tuner, 1937, 14".. **$4,000+**

Model 180 Tabletop Television

DuMont, Model 180, tabletop model, 1939, 14" (ILLUS.) **$8,000**

DuMont Model 183 Console TV

DuMont, Model 183, console model, 1939, 14" (ILLUS.).. **$10,000**

Model RA-101 Wall Installation

DuMont, Model RA-101, custom model for
wall installation, 1946, 20" (ILLUS., top of
page) **$1,000**

DuMont, Model RA-101, "Plymouth," wood-
en console w/Early American styled cab-
inet, 1948 .... **$45**

DuMont Model RA-101-1A Console with Motorized Screen & Radio & Phonograph

Model RA-102 Console Model

DuMont, Model RA-101-1A, console model w/motorized screen & radio & phonograph, 1946, 20" (ILLUS., bottom of previous page)... **$1,500**

DuMont, Model RA-102, Clifton console model, 1947, 12" (ILLUS., above)........... **$1,200**

DuMont Model RA-103 Tabletop

DuMont, Model RA-103, Chatham trapezoi-
dal wooden "dog house"-shaped tabletop
model, 1947, 12" (ILLUS., top of page)
.... **$300-400**

DuMont, Model RA-103, Savoy wooden
console model, 1947, 12" (ILLUS., bot-
tom of page).. **$150**

Handsome DuMont RA-103 Savoy Model

DuMont Green Manchu Console TV

DuMont, Model RA-103-D3, square table-top model, 1947, 12" **$200**

DuMont, Model RA-105, dark green & black Manchu console model, 1949, 20" (ILLUS., top of page) **$500**

DuMont, Model RA-105, large square table-top model, 1949, 12" (ILLUS., bottom of page) **$150**

DuMont Model RA-105 Table Model

DuMont RA-108 Console Model

DuMont, Model RA-108, console model w/continuous tuning, 1949, 20" (ILLUS., top of page) **$100**

DuMont, Model RA-109, console model w/radio, 1950, 19" **$100**

DuMont, Model RA-111, console model w/radio, metal grillework over cloth speaker, molded flat base, 1950, 15" (ILLUS., top next page) **$175**

DuMont, Model RA-112, console model w/radio, 1950, 15" (ILLUS., bottom next page) **$75-100**

DuMont, Model RA-113, interestingly styled wooden console, ca. 1950, 15" **$125**

DuMont, Model RA-115, large wooden tabletop model, 1951, 15" **$75**

DuMont Model RA-111 Large Console

DuMont Model RA-112 Console Model

DuMont "Royal Sovereign" Model

DuMont, Model RA-119, "Royal Sovereign" console model, 1951, 30" (ILLUS., top of page) **$2,500**
DuMont, Model RA-160, large-screen console model w/FM radio, 1950s **$75**
Electro-Technical Industries, Model 10-A, kit TV w/no cabinet, 1948, 10" **$500**
Electro-Technical Industries, Model 12-B, kit TV, wooden tabletop, 1949, 12" **$450**
Electro-Technical Industries, Model T-7, kit TV w/no cabinet, 1948, 7" **$500**
Electro-Technical Industries, Model T-8, kit TV, wooden tabletop, 1949, 8" **$800**
Electromatic, Model 101, wooden tabletop model, 1949, 10" (ILLUS., next column) **$800**

Electromatic Model 101 Wood Tabletop TV

Emerson Model 508 Pop-up Console

Emerson, Model 508, wooden console model w/a pop-up screen, late 1940s, 16" (ILLUS., top of page)................................. **$350**

Emerson, Model 527, wooden console model w/sloped front, 1948, 10" **$700**
Emerson, Model 545, wooden tabletop, 1948, 10"... **$500**

Emerson Model 571 Wooden Tabletop

Emerson Model 600 Portable TV in Leatherette Case

Emerson, Model 571, wooden tabletop, 1948, 10" (ILLUS., bottom previous page) **$250**

Emerson, Model 585, wooden console model w/radio & phonograph, double doors, 1949, 10" **$100**

Emerson, Model 600, portable w/leatherette case, 1949, 7" (ILLUS., top of page) ... **$150**

Emerson, Model 606, wooden console model w/four knobs below the screen, ca. 1949 .... **$55**

Emerson, Model 608, wooden console model w/pop-up screen, 1949, 16" (ILLUS., bottom of page)........................... **$400**

Emerson Model 608 Console with Pop-up Screen

Emerson Model 609 Projection Console

Emerson, Model 609, wooden console projection model, 1949 (ILLUS.)... **$225**

Emerson Model 610 Rectangular Wooden Tabletop TV

Emerson, Model 610, rectangular wooden tabletop w/golden front grille, 1949, 7" (ILLUS.) **$150**

Emerson Model 611 Wooden Tabletop TV

Emerson, Model 611, rectangular wooden tabletop w/four knobs below screen, 1949, 10" (ILLUS., top of page) **$175**

Emerson, Model 614, tabletop w/Bakelite case, 1949, 10" (ILLUS., bottom of page) **$140**

Emerson, Model 619, wooden console model, 1949, 10" **$100**

Emerson, Model 621, wooden tabletop, 1949, 10" **$130**

Emerson, Model 622, wooden console model w/radio & phonograph, 1949, 10".... **$100**

Emerson, Model 624, wooden tabletop, 1949, 10" **$160**

Emerson, Model 626, wooden console model, 1949, 16" **$100**

Emerson Model 614 Bakelite Tabletop Set from 1949

Emerson Model 628 Wood Tabletop TV with AM/FM Radio

Emerson, Model 628, wooden tabletop w/AM/FM radio, slide rule tuning, 1949, 10" (ILLUS., top of page) **$200**

Emerson, Model 629, wooden console model, 1949, 16" **$75**

Emerson, Model 630, wooden console model w/radio & phonograph, 1950, 12".... **$100**

Emerson, Model 631, wooden tabletop, 1950, 16" **$140**

Emerson, Model 633, wooden console model w/double doors, 1950, 16" **$75**

Emerson, Model 637, wooden tabletop, 1950, 10" **$150**

Emerson, Model 639, wooden portable, 1950, 7" **$150**

Emerson, Model 644, wooden tabletop, 1950, 12" **$125**

Emerson, Model 647, wooden console model, 1950, 12" **$75**

Emerson, Model 648, tabletop w/Bakelite case, 1950, 10" (ILLUS., bottom of page) **$175**

Emerson Model 648 Bakelite Tabletop TV from 1950

Emerson Model 649 Projection TV

Emerson, Model 649, dark wood console projection model, 1950 (ILLUS., top of page) **$125**

Emerson, Model 650, wooden tabletop, 1950, 12" **$150**

Emerson, Model 651, wooden tabletop, 1950, 16" **$125**

Emerson, Model 654, wooden console model, 1950, 12" **$75**

Emerson, Model 662, tabletop w/Bakelite case, 1951, 14" **$75**

Emerson, Model 663, wooden tabletop, 1951, 14" **$75**

Emerson, Model 666, wooden console model w/radio & phonograph, 1951, 16" **$50**

Espey, "Image" kit TV, large flat metal front w/small round screen & speaker above rows of seven knobs, 1947, 3" (ILLUS., bottom of page) **$700**

FADA, Model 799, wooden tabletop, 1948, 10" **$300**

1947 Espey "Image" Kit Television

Unusual FADA Model 880 Projection Set

FADA, Model 880, unusual projection set w/stepped top, 1948 (ILLUS.) **$450**

FADA, Model 895, wooden console w/radio & phonograph, double doors, 1948, 12" **$125**

FADA, Model 899, wooden tabletop, 1948, 10" **$250**

FADA, Model 925, wooden tabletop, 1948, 16" **$200**

FADA, Model 930, wooden tabletop, 1948, 12" **$225**

FADA, Model 940, wooden console model, 1948, 12" **$125**

FADA, Model R-1050, wooden tabletop, 1950, 16" **$100**

FADA, Model S-1030, wooden tabletop, 1950, 12" **$150**

FADA, Model S-1050, wooden tabletop, 1949, 12" **$150**

FADA, Model TV-30, wooden tabletop model w/stepped case, center screen flanked by cloth speaker panels above the knobs, 1947, 10" (ILLUS., bottom of page) **$400**

Firestone, Model 13-G-3, wooden tabletop, 1948, 7" **$250**

Firestone, Model 13-G-33, tabletop w/leatherette case, 1948, 7" **$220**

Firestone, Model 13-G-4, wooden tabletop, 1948, 10" **$200**

Firestone, Model 13-G-5, wooden console model, 1948, 10" **$120**

Freed Eisemann, Model 54, wooden console model, 1949, 16" **$125**

Freed Eisemann, Model 55, wooden console model, 1949, 16" **$125**

Freed Eisemann, Model 56, wooden console model, 1949, 16" **$125**

Freed Eisemann, Model 77, wooden tabletop, 1949, 16" **$200**

Garod, Model 1000TV, wooden tabletop model w/radio, 1948, 12" **$300**

Garod, Model 1000TVP, wooden console model w/radio & phonograph, 1948, 12".... **$200**

Garod, Model 1020TV, wooden tabletop model w/radio, 1948, 12" **$300**

Garod, Model 1021TVP, wooden console model w/radio & phonograph, 1948, 12".... **$200**

Garod, Model 1030TV, blond wood tabletop model w/radio, 1948, 12" **$300**

Garod, Model 1042G, wooden tabletop, 1949, 10" **$200**

Garod, Model 1043G, blond wood tabletop, 1949, 10" **$225**

FADA Model TV-30 Tabletop TV with Stepped Wood Case

Garod Model 10TZ20 Tabletop with Radio

Garod, Model 10TZ20, mahogany wood tabletop model w/radio, 1949, 10" (ILLUS., top of page) **$300**

Garod, Model 10TZ21, blond wood tabletop model w/radio, 1949, 10" **$350**

Garod, Model 10TZ22, wooden console model w/radio, 1949, 10" **$200**

Garod, Model 10TZ23, blond wood console model w/radio, 1949, 10" **$250**

Garod, Model 1244G, wooden tabletop, 1949, 12" **$200**

Garod, Model 1245G, blond wood tabletop, 1949, 12" **$225**

Garod, Model 12TZ20, wooden tabletop w/radio, 1949, 12" **$200**

Garod, Model 12TZ21, blond wood tabletop model w/radio, 1949, 12" **$300**

Garod, Model 12TZ22, wooden console model w/radio, 1949, 12" **$200**

Garod, Model 12TZ23, blond wood console model w/radio, 1949, 12" **$250**

Garod, Model 1546G, wooden tabletop, 1949, 16" **$175**

Garod, Model 1547G, blond wood tabletop, 1949, 16" **$200**

Garod, Model 1548G, wooden console model, 1949, 16" **$150**

Garod, Model 1549G, blond wood console model, 1949, 16" **$175**

Garod Model 930TV Tabletop Set with AM/FM Radio

General Electric Model 10T4 Tabletop TV

Garod, Model 15TZ24, wooden console model w/radio, 1949, 15" **$200**

Garod, Model 15TZ25, blond wood tabletop model w/radio, 1949, 15" **$250**

Garod, Model 15TZ26, wooden console model w/radio, 1949, 15" **$200**

Garod, Model 1672, wooden console model, 1950, 16" **$125**

Garod, Model 1673, blond wood console model, 1950, 16" **$150**

Garod, Model 1974, wooden console model, 1950, 19" **$75**

Garod, Model 1975, wooden console model, 1950, 19" **$75**

Garod, Model 900TV, wooden tabletop, 1948, 10" **$400**

Garod, Model 910TV, blond wood tabletop model, 1948, 10" **$500**

Garod, Model 920TV, wooden tabletop, 1948, 10" **$350**

Garod, Model 921TV, wooden console model w/radio & phonograph, 1948, 10" **$200**

Garod, Model 930TV, tabletop model w/AM/FM radio, 1949, 10" (ILLUS., bottom previous page) **$400**

General Electric, Model 10C101, wooden console model, 1949, 10" **$75**

General Electric, Model 10C102, blond wood console model, 1949, 10" **$100**

General Electric, Model 10T1, tabletop w/streamlined Bakelite case, 1948, 10" **$250**

General Electric, Model 10T4, wooden tabletop with brass grille & knobs below the screen, 1949, 10" (ILLUS., top of page) **$200**

General Electric, Model 10T6, tabletop w/Bakelite case, 1949, 10" **$200**

General Electric, Model 12C101, wooden console model, 1949, 12" **$75**

General Electric, Model 12C102, blond wood console model, 1949, 12" **$100**

General Electric, Model 12C109, wooden console model w/double doors, 1949, 12" **$75**

General Electric, Model 12K1, wooden console model w/radio & phonograph, 1949 .... **$75**

General Electric, Model 12T1, wooden tabletop w/very square corners, 1949, 12" **$150**

General Electric, Model 12T3, wooden tabletop, 1949, 12" **$150**

General Electric, Model 12T4, blond wood tabletop, 1949, 12" **$175**

General Electric, Model 12T7, wooden tabletop, 1949, 12" **$150**

General Electric, Model 14T, portable w/painted metal cabinet, 1950s **$65**

General Electric Model 800 Tabletop

General Electric, Model 800, tabletop model w/Bakelite case, 1949, 10" (ILLUS.) **$300**

General Electric Model 801 Console with Radio & Screen Behind Doors

GE Model 802 Tall Console Combination

General Electric, Model 801, console model w/radio, screen & large AM dial behind small doors, 1947, 10" (ILLUS., bottom previous page) **$350**

General Electric, Model 802, console model w/radio & phonograph behind large doors, 1947, 10" (ILLUS., top of page) **$300**

General Electric, Model 803, wooden tabletop model w/radio, domed top w/speaker panel at front under cloth & metal lattice, 1948, 10" (ILLUS., bottom of page)... **$350-400**

General Electric Model 803 Tabletop Set

General Electric Model 806 Tabletop Set

General Electric, Model 806, tall wooden tabletop w/glass front plate, 1949, 10" (ILLUS.)..................... **$200**

GE Model 807 Blond Wood Tabletop Set

General Electric, Model 807, blond wood tabletop model w/glass front plate, 1949, 10" (ILLUS.).......... **$200**

General Electric Model 810 Table Model

General Electric, Model 810, wide wooden
  tabletop, 1949, 10" (ILLUS., top of page)
  .... **$225**
General Electric, Model 812, square wood
  tabletop model, 1950, 12" **$50**

General Electric, Model 813, wooden
  tabletop, 1949, 10"..................................... **$175**
General Electric, Model 814, wooden
  tabletop, 1949, 10"..................................... **$150**

Large GE Model 90 Console with Radio & a Long Mirror in the Lid

Handsome GE Model 901 Console Projection Set with Radio & Phonograph

General Electric, Model 815, wooden
tabletop, 1949, 10".................................. **$150**
General Electric, Model 817, wooden con-
sole model, 1949, 12" **$100**
General Electric, Model 818, wooden con-
sole model w/radio & phonograph, 1949,
12"... **$75**
General Electric, Model 820, blond wood
console model w/radio & phonograph,
1949, 12"... **$100**
General Electric, Model 821, wooden ta-
bletop, 1949, 12"..................................... **$150**
General Electric, Model 830, wooden ta-
bletop, 1949, 12"..................................... **$150**

General Electric, Model 835, wooden ta-
bletop, 1949, 10"..................................... **$150**
General Electric, Model 90, console model
w/long mirror in lid & radio, 1940, 12"
(ILLUS., bottom of previous page)........ **$15,000**
General Electric, Model 901, wooden console projection model w/radio & phono-
graph, 1947 (ILLUS., top of page) **$600**
General Electric, Model 9T001, tabletop
model w/metal case, 1956, 10".................... **$50**
General Electric, Model HM-171, wooden
tabletop model w/three-channel pushbutton tuning, 1939, 5" (ILLUS., bottom of
page).. **$8,000**

Rare GE Model HM-171 Tabletop Set from 1939

Extremely Rare GE HM-185 Tall Console Set from 1939

General Electric, Model HM-185, wooden console model, the small screen above a row of knobs over the lower case w/wide louvers, 1939, 5" (ILLUS.).. **$12,000**

Extraordinarily Rare Early General Electric 1939 Console TV

General Electric, Model HM-225, tall wooden console model w/three wide bands of speaker cloth wrapping around the lower front, 1939, 10" (ILLUS.) **$15,000**

Rare GE Model HM-226 Fancy Wooden Console with Doors, made in 1939

Extremely Rare 1939 GE Model HM-275 Wood Console TV-Radio

General Electric, Model HM-226, wooden console model w/radio & wooden doors on the upper half, 1939, 12" (ILLUS., bottom previous page) **$15,000**

General Electric, Model HM-275, dark wood console model w/mirror in the long lid & a radio, 1939, 12" (ILLUS., top of page)... **$18,000**

1976 General Electric Plastic Portable

General Electric, Model XB-2454, portable model in a red, white & blue plastic cabinet, 1976 (ILLUS.)
.... **$45**

1949 Grinnell Wooden Tabletop Television

Grinnell, rectangular wooden tabletop model, 1949, 10" (ILLUS., top of page)............. **$150**

Hallicrafters, Model 509, wooden tabletop model w/pushbutton tuning, 1949, 10"....... **$350**

Hallicrafters, Model 510, tabletop model in Bakelite case w/pushbutton tuning, 1949, 10".. **$300**

Hallicrafters, Model 512, wooden console model, 1949, 12"....................................... **$100**

Hallicrafters, Model 514, portable model in leatherette case, 1948, 7" **$400**

Hallicrafters, Model 515, wooden console model, 1949, 15"....................................... **$100**

Hallicrafters, Model 600, rectangular wooden tabletop set w/three large knobs, 1949, 10" (ILLUS., bottom of page) **$150**

Hallicrafters, Model 715, tabletop model in a Bakelite case, 1950, 12" **$100**

Hallicrafters, Model 716, tabletop model w/leatherette case, 1950, 12" **$100**

Hallicrafters, Model T-505, blond wood tabletop model w/thirteen-channel pushbutton tuning, 1949, 7".............................. **$400**

Hallicrafters, Model T-505, wooden tabletop model w/thirteen-channel pushbutton tuning, 1949, 7".. **$350**

Hallicrafters, Model T-506, wooden tabletop model w/thirteen-channel pushbutton tuning, 1949, 7".. **$350**

Simple Hallicrafters Model 600 TV Set

Hallicrafters Model T-54 Table Model

Hallicrafters, Model T-54, tabletop model in metal case w/thirteen-channel pushbutton tuning, designed by Raymond Lowey, 1948, 7" (ILLUS., top of page) **$400-450**

Hallicrafters, Model T-54, tabletop model in metal case w/twelve-channel pushbutton tuning, 1948, 7" **$350-400**

Hallicrafters, Model T-60, tabletop model in Bakelite case w/pushbutton turning, 1949, 7" **$300**

Hallicrafters, Model T-67, wooden tabletop model w/pushbutton tuning, 1949, 10" **$250**

Hallicrafters, Model T-68, wooden projection console model, 1949 .... **$300**

Hoffman, Colorcaster color console model, 1954, 19" (ILLUS., top next page)........... **$6,000**

Hoffman, Model 600, blond wood tabletop model, 1949, 10" **$225**

Hoffman, Model 601, wooden tabletop, 1949, 12" **$200**

Hoffman, Model 610, blond wood tabletop model w/double doors, 1949, 10" **$250**

Hoffman, Model 611, wooden tabletop model w/double doors, 1949, 10" **$225**

Hoffman, Model 612, wooden tabletop model w/double doors, 1949, 12" **$200**

Hoffman, Model 613, blond wood tabletop model w/double doors, 1949, 12" **$225**

Hoffman, Model 841, blond wood console model w/radio, double doors, 1949, 12" **$100**

Hoffman, Model 842, wooden console model w/radio & double doors, 1949, 12" **$75**

Hoffman, Model 843, wooden console model w/radio & double doors, 1949, 12" **$75**

Hoffman, Model 914, blond wood console model w/radio & phonograph & double doors, 1949, 12" **$100**

Hoffman, Model 915, wooden console model w/radio & phonograph, double doors, 1949, 12" **$75**

Hotel-Vision, wooden tabletop model w/six-channel pushbutton tuning, 1949, 10" **$350**

Jackson Industries, Model 5000, wooden tabletop, 1949, 10" **$300**

Jackson Industries, Model 5050, wooden console model, 1949, 10" **$150**

Jackson Industries, Model 5200, wooden tabletop, 1949, 12" **$275**

Jackson Industries, Model 5350, wooden console model, 1949, 12" **$125**

1954 Hoffman Colorcaster Color Console Model Television

Jenkins, Model 100 mechanical set w/scanning disk, no cabinet, 1931 (ILLUS., top next page) **$5,000**

Jenkins, Model R-400, mechanical set w/scanning disk & lens for projecting image, 1931 .... **$8,000**

JVC, Model 3100D Video Capsule, pyramid-shaped plastic, 1978 .... **$400**

JVC, Model 3240, Videosphere, 1979, 9" **$200**

Kaye Halbert, Model 924, dark wood tabletop model w/heavy molding framing the raised screen, 1949, 12" (ILLUS., bottom next page) **$200**

Rare 1931 Jenkins Model 100 Set

Kaye Halbert Model 924

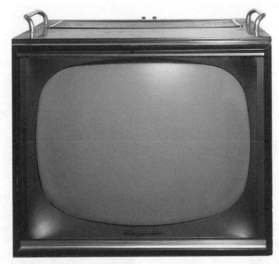

Magnavox Model MV-119 Table Model

Magnavox, Model MV-119, square wooden tabletop model w/controls under a top wooden panel, ca. 1960s (ILLUS., top of page) **$30**

Majestic, Model 12C4, wooden console model, 1950, 12" **$50**

Majestic, Model 12T2, wooden tabletop, 1950, 12" **$100**

Majestic, Model 16T2, wooden tabletop model w/Bakelite front, 1950, 14" **$125**

Majestic, Model 18C91, wooden console model w/radio, double doors at the top & bottom, 1948, 7" (ILLUS., bottom of page) **$600**

Majestic, Model 7TV850, wooden tabletop, 1948, 7" **$250**

Meck, Model XA-701, wooden tabletop, 1948 .... **$375**

Meck, Model XB-702, wooden tabletop, 1948, 7" **$400**

Meck, Model XC-703, portable in leatherette case, 1948, 7" **$400**

Meck, Model XL-750, wooden tabletop, 1949, 10" **$250**

Meck, Model XN-752, wooden console model, 1949, 10" **$150**

Meck, Model XQ-776, wooden tabletop, 1949, 12" **$200**

Majestic Model 18C91 Large Console TV from 1948

Early Meissner Metal Kit Television

Meissner, Model 10-1153, metal kit TV w/no cabinet, 1939 (ILLUS., top of page) **$4,500**

Meissner, Model TV-1, kit TV w/wooden cabinet, 1948, 10" **$500**

Meissner, Model TV-24, kit TV w/wooden cabinet, 1948, 12" **$450**

Motorola, Model 10T3, wooden tabletop, 1949, 10" **$150**

Motorola, Model 10VK12, wooden console model, 1949, 10" **$100**

Motorola, Model 10VK9, wooden console model, 1949, 10" **$100**

Motorola, Model 10VT1, wooden tabletop, 1949, 10" **$150**

Motorola, Model 10VT3, blond wood table-top model, 1949, 10" **$175**

Motorola, Model 12VK15, wooden console model, 1950, 12" **$75**

Motorola, Model 12VK18, wooden console model, 1949, 12" **$125**

Motorola, Model 12VK18B, blond wood console model, 1949, 12" **$150**

Motorola, Model 12VT13, wooden tabletop, 1950, 12" **$100**

Motorola, Model 14K1, simple wooden console model, 1950... **$50**

Motorola, Model 17T5, tabletop model in a Bakelite cabinet, ca. 1950, 17" **$50**

Rare Motorola Color Console from 1954

Motorola, Model 19CK2, color console model w/21" CRT, 1954 (ILLUS., top of page).. **$4,000**

Motorola, Model 19CT1, color console model w/19" CRT, 1954 (ILLUS., bottom of page).. **$4,500**

Motorola, Model 19P1, "Astronaut" large transistor model portable, 1960, 19" **$125**

Motorola, Model 21-CS, wooden console model on four legs, 1950s, 21" **$50**

Motorola, Model 21K79, Moderne-style wooden console w/lower built-in shelf, 1957... **$125**

Motorola, Model 21T32, tabletop set in metal cabinet, 1957, 21" **$35**

Rare Motorola Model 19CT1 Color Console TV from 1954

Motorola Portable TV in Leatherette Suitcase-style Cabinet

Motorola, Model 21T8, wooden tabletop model w/large screen, 1950s **$35**

Motorola, Model 7VT-5, portable leatherette suitcase model w/antenna, 1948, 7" (ILLUS., top of page)................................. **$300**

Motorola, Model 7VT2, tabletop model w/Bakelite case, 1949, 7"........................... **$250**

Motorola, Model 7VT2W, tabletop model w/Bakelite case painted white, 1949, 7" **$250**

Motorola, Model 9L1, portable model in red leatherette case, 1949, 8" **$200**

Motorola, Model 9T1, low rectangular tabletop model in Bakelite case, 1948, 7" (ILLUS., bottom of page)............................ **$200**

Motorola, Model 9VT1, wooden tabletop, 1949, 8"... **$200**

Motorola, Model VF-102, wooden console model w/radio & phonograph, 1948, 10".... **$150**

Motorola, Model VK-101, wooden console model w/AM/FM drop-down radio, 1948 .... **$250**

Motorola, Model VK-106, wooden console model, 1948, 10"....................................... **$125**

Motorola, Model VK-106B, blond wood console model, 1948, 10" **$150**

Motorola Model 9T1 Rectangular Tabletop TV from 1948

Motorola Model VT-105 1948 Tabletop

Motorola, Model VT-105, wooden tabletop model w/stepped top, 1948, 10" (ILLUS., top of page) **$400**

Motorola, Model VT-107, wooden tabletop, 1948, 10" **$275**

Motorola, Model VT-107B, blond wood tabletop model, 1848, 10" **$275**

Motorola, Model VT-71, wooden tabletop w/wide metal grille across the front, 1948, 7" (ILLUS., bottom of page) **$150**

Motorola, Model VT-73, cloth-covered portable model w/antenna, 1948, 7" **$275**

Motorola Model VT-71 Wooden Tabletop with Metal Grille

1960s Wide Wooden Motorola Console Set

Motorola, wide wooden console model w/slender canted legs, 1960s (ILLUS., top of page)... **$75**

Muntz, Model 17A3A, wooden tabletop, 1951, 17" (ILLUS., bottom of page) **$100**

Muntz, Model 17PL, "Holiday," portable in a plastic & metal cabinet, ca. 1959, 17" **$25**

Muntz, Model 23EA, "Early American Lowboy," wooden console on four carved legs, 1961... **$30**

Muntz, Model CP-2, "Capri," console w/a wide TV screen & radio on the front, a phonograph built in to the top, raised on four pointed metal legs, 1958...................... **$85**

Muntz, Model M1, blond wood console model, 1949, 12"....................................... **$175**

Muntz, Model M1, wooden console model, 1949, 12".. **$150**

Muntz, Model M30, wooden tabletop, 1950, 12".. **$200**

Muntz, Model M31R, wooden console model, 1950, 16".. **$60**

1951 Muntz Model 17A3A Tabletop TV

National Model TV-10 Wooden Tabletop TV in Stepped Cabinet

National, Model TV-10, wooden tabletop
w/stepped cabinet, 1949, 10" (ILLUS.,
top of page) **$250**
National, Model TV-12, wooden tabletop,
1949, 12" **$250**
National, Model TV-1201, wooden tabletop,
1949, 12" **$200**
National, Model TV-1225, wooden console
model, 1949, 12" **$100**

National, Model TV-1601, wooden tabletop,
1949, 16" **$175**
National, Model TV-1625, wooden console
model, 1949, 16" **$100**
National, Model TV-7, tabletop model
w/metal case, 1949, 7" **$400**
National, Model TV-7M, tabletop model
w/low rectangular metal case w/meter,
1949, 7" (ILLUS., bottom of page) **$700**

Unusual National Model TV-7M Tabletop Set in Metal Case

National Model TV-7W Wooden Tabletop TV from 1949

National, Model TV-7W, rectangular wooden tabletop w/speaker grilles flanking the small central screen, 1949, 7" (ILLUS., top of page) **$300**

Neilson, Model 1010, wooden tabletop, 1949, 710 .... **$275**

Neilson, Model 1018, wooden console model, 1949, 10" **$125**

Norelco, Model PA-2A, Duo-View projection adapter, 1948 (ILLUS., bottom of page) **$200**

Norelco, Model PT-200, wooden projection console model, 1948 .... **$150**

Norelco, Model PT-300, wooden projection console model w/double doors, 1948 .... **$150**

Norelco Duo-View Projection Adapter

1953 Olympic Fancy Console TV with Radio & Phonograph

Olympic, console model in fancy Colonial Revival blond wood cabinet w/radio & phonograph, 1953 (ILLUS.)........................ **$100**

Olympic, Model 928, wooden console model w/mirror in lid & radio & phonograph, 1948, 10" (ILLUS., bottom of page) **$350**

Olympic, Model DX-214, wooden tabletop, 1949, 12" **$150**

Olympic, Model DX-215, wooden console model w/double doors, 1949, 12" **$75**

Olympic, Model DX-619, wooden console model w/double doors, 1950, 16" **$50**

Olympic, Model DX-950, wooden tabletop, 1950, 16"... **$125**

Olympic Model 928 Wooden Console with Radio & Phonograph

Olympic Tabletop "Duplicator" Set

Olympic, Model RTU-3, "Duplicator," wooden tabletop monitor, 1949 (ILLUS., top of page) **$225**
Olympic, Model TV-104, wooden tabletop, 1948, 10" **$200**
Olympic, Model TV-105, wooden console model, 1948, 10" **$100**
Olympic, Model TV-106, wooden tabletop, 1948, 10" **$200**
Olympic, Model TV-107, wooden tabletop, 1948, 10" **$200**
Olympic, Model TV-108, wooden tabletop, 1948, 10" **$200**
Olympic, Model TV-922, wooden tabletop, 1948, 10" **$200**
Olympic, Model TV-922, wooden tabletop 1949, 12" **$150**
Olympic, Model TV-922L, wooden tabletop, 1948, 10" **$225**
Olympic, Model TV-928, wooden console model, mirror in lid, w/radio & phonograph **$350**
Olympic, Model TV-944, wooden tabletop, 1949, 12" **$175**

Packard Bell, Model 1080TV, blond wood console model w/radio & phonograph, 1949, 10" **$100**
Packard Bell, Model 2001TV, blond wood tabletop model, 1949, 12" **$225**
Packard Bell, Model 2002TV, blond wood console model, 1949, 12" **$100**
Packard Bell, Model 2091, wooden tabletop, 1949, 12" **$200**
Packard Bell, Model 2092TV, wooden console model, 1949, 12" **$80**
Packard Bell, Model 2292TV, blond wood consolette, 1949, 10" **$125**
Packard Bell, Model 2293TV, wooden tabletop, 1949, 10" **$200**
Packard Bell, Model 2294TV, wooden tabletop, 1949, 12" **$175**
Packard Bell, Model 3193TV, wooden tabletop, 1949, 10" **$200**
Packard Bell, Model 4580, wooden console model w/radio, phonograph & phonograph recorder, 1948, 12" **$350**
Panasonic, Model CT-101, 1 1/2" LCD, 1980 .... **$300**

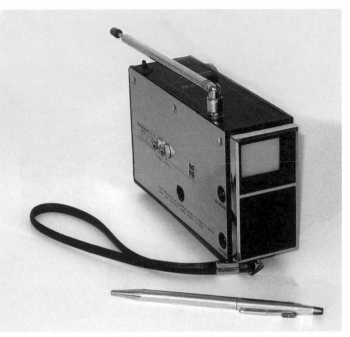

Panasonic 1971 Model TR-001 Small Portable TV

Panasonic, Model TR-001, 1 1/2" plastic portable set, small rectangular case w/strap handle, 1971 (ILLUS., top of page) **$500**

Panasonic, Model TR-003, 3" plastic model w/radio, 1975... **$150**

Panasonic, Model TR-005, "Flying Saucer" model, 1975, 5" (ILLUS., bottom of page) **$600**

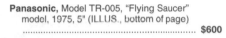

Panasonic "Flying Saucer" Television

Panasonic 1981 Model TR-1010P Small Portable TV

Panasonic, Model TR-1010P, portable set in low & wide rectangular plastic case w/strap handle, 1981, 1 1/2"(ILLUS., top of page)... **$100**

Panasonic, Model TR-535, pop-up style model, 1977, 5".. **$60**

Pathe, Model 12-1, wooden tabletop, 1948, 12"... **$500**

Phaostron, Model P-18-C, "Magic Lantern" console model, 1949, 12" (ILLUS., bottom of page).. **$150**

Philco, Model 2125, tabletop model in grain-painted cabinet, ca. 1953, 20" **$45**

Philco, Model 2271, "Colonial" style wooden console w/double doors, 21", 1952......... **$55**

Phaostron "Magic Lantern" Console TV from 1949

Philco Model 48-1000 Tabletop TV with Offset Screen

Philco, Model 48-1000, wooden tabletop model w/offset screen, 1948, 10" (ILLUS.)...................... **$400-450**

Philco Model 48-1001 Wooden Tabletop TV with Arched Top

Philco, Model 48-1001, wooden tabletop w/arched top, 1948, 10" (ILLUS.) **$250**

Philco Model 48-1050 Console TV

Philco, Model 48-1050, wooden console model w/long speakers flanking the screen & knobs, 1948, 10" (ILLUS., top of page) **$100**

Philco, Model 48-2500, console projection set, 1948 .... **$200**

Philco, Model 48-700, tabletop model in Bakelite case, 1948, 7" (ILLUS., bottom of page) **$300**

Philco, Model 49-1002, wooden tabletop, 1949, 10" **$200**

Philco, Model 49-1040, wooden consolette, 1949, 10" **$250**

Philco, Model 49-1077, wooden console model w/radio & phonograph, 1949, 10" **$100**

Philco Model 48-700 Bakelite Tabletop TV from 1948

Philco Model 49-1150 Consolette TV

Philco, Model 49-1150, wooden consolette, raised on square tapering legs, 1949, 12" (ILLUS., top of page).................................. **$225**

Philco, Model 49-1240, wooden consolette, 1949, 12".. **$225**

Philco, Model 49-1278, console model w/radio & phonograph, 1949, 12" (ILLUS., bottom of page)........................... **$100**

Philco Model 49-1278 Console Set

Philco Model 49-702

Philco, Model 49-1280, wooden console model w/double doors, 1949, 12".............. **$100**

Philco, Model 49-702, wooden tabletop, 1949, 7" (ILLUS., top of page) **$250**

Philco, Model 50-700, wide wooden tabletop model, 1950, 7"................................... **$450**

Philco, Model 50-701, tabletop model in Bakelite case, 1950, 7" (ILLUS., bottom of page).. **$250-375**

Philco Model 50-701 Bakelite Tabletop TV from 1950

Philco Model 50-702 Tabletop TV

Philco, Model 50-702, wooden tabletop w/arched top, 1950, 7" (ILLUS., top of page) **$375**

Philco, Model 50-T-1104, tabletop model in a Bakelite case, 1950, 10" **$175**

Philco, Model 50-T-1105, wooden tabletop, 1950, 10" **$150**

Philco, Model 50-T-1403, round-topped wooden tabletop, 1950, 12" (ILLUS., bottom of page) **$125-150**

Philco, Model 50-T-1404, wooden tabletop, 1950, 12" **$150**

Philco, Model 50-T-1443, wooden console model, 1950, 14" **$100**

Philco, Model 50-T-702, wooden tabletop model, 1949, 7" **$75**

Philco, Model 51-PT-1207, wooden tabletop, 1950, 10" **$75**

Round-topped Philco Model 50-T1403

Philco 1951 TV in Metal Cabinet on Stand

Philco, Model 51-T-1601, tabletop in metal cabinet, 1951, 16" (ILLUS. on separate stand) **$80**

Philco "Safari" Transistor Television

Philco, Model H2010, "Safari," first transistor TV, 1959 (ILLUS.) **$150-175**

Philco Model TV-123 Color Console TV from 1956

Philco, Model TV-123, color console model, 1956, 21" (ILLUS., top of page) **$800**

Philco, Model UG-3408, "Predicta Debutante" model, 1960, 17" **$500**

Philco, Model UG-3410, "Predicta Princess" model, 1960, 17" **$500**

Philco, Model UG-3412, "Predicta Siesta" model, 1960, 17" **$500**

Philco, Model UG-4242, "Predicta Holiday" tabletop model, 1958, 21" (ILLUS., bottom of page)... **$400**

Philco Predicta Holiday Model Tabletop TV

Philco Barber Pole-style "Predicta" Set

Philco, Model UG-4654, "Predicta" barber pole-style blond wood console model, 1958, 21".. **$800**

Philco, Model UG-4654, "Predicta" barber pole-style wooden console model, 1958, 21" (ILLUS., top of page) **$600**

Philco, Model UG-4659, "Predicta Miss America" wooden console model, 1960, 21"... **$150**

Philco, Model UG-4720, "Predicta Tandem" model, 1958, 21" (ILLUS., bottom of page).. **$1,200**

Modernistic Philco "Predicta Tandem" Tabletop TV from 1958

Unusual Philco Predicta Continental Set

Philco, Model UG-4730, "Predicta Continental" wooden console model on pedestal base w/wing-like legs, 1960, 21" (ILLUS., top of page)................................. **$800**

Pilot, Model TV-125, rectangular wooden tabletop, 1949, 12" (ILLUS., bottom of page)... **$200**
Pilot, Model TV-161, wooden tabletop, 1950, 16"... **$150**

Pilot Model TV-125 Rectangular Wooden Tabletop Set from 1949

Pilot Model TV-37 Tabletop TV in Press-board Cabinet

Pilot, Model TV-37, tabletop model wood press-board cabinet, 1947, 3" (ILLUS., top of page).. **$350**

Pilot, Model TV-950, wooden projection console model, 1950................................. **$200**

Radio Craftsman, Model RC-101, custom chassis, no cabinet, 1948, 16" (ILLUS., bottom of page).. **$150**

Radio Craftsman Model RC-101 Custom Chassis

Radio Craftsman Model RC-200 Wooden Console with Chrome Chassis

Radio Craftsman, Model RC-200, wooden two-door console model w/chrome chassis, 1950, 16"-24" (ILLUS., top of page) **$125**

RCA, Berkshire Breakfront console projection model w/radio & phonograph, 1948 .... **$3,500**

RCA, Berkshire Regency console projection model w/radio & phonograph, 1948 .... **$2,500**

RCA, Model 14-PD-3030, portable w/metal cabinet, 1954, 14" **$100**

RCA, Model 14S7072, portable in black metal cabinet w/carrying handle, square screen, 1957 .... **$25**

RCA, Model 17-PD-8096, portable w/metal cabinet, 1954, 17" (ILLUS., bottom of page) **$100**

RCA, Model 17S602, "Thifton," simple portable tabletop set, mid-1950s, 17" **$20**

RCA, Model 17T-172, "Covington," console model, 1956, 17" **$55**

RCA, Model 17T151, "Glenside," portable w/blond wood-painted metal cabinet, 17" **$70**

RCA Model 17-PD Portable in Metal Cabinet

RCA Model 21-CT-55 Color Console TV

RCA, Model 21-CT-55, color console model, 1955, 21" (ILLUS., top of page).......... **$1,000**
RCA, Model 21-T-178, "Rockingham," console model, mid-1950s, 21"......................... **$35**
RCA, Model 21S, wooden console model, 1953, 21".. **$50**

RCA, Model 21T, blond wood console model w/lattice grille across the lower front, 1953, 21" (ILLUS., bottom of page) **$50-75**
RCA, Model 2T51, tabletop model in metal cabinet, 1950, 12" **$100**

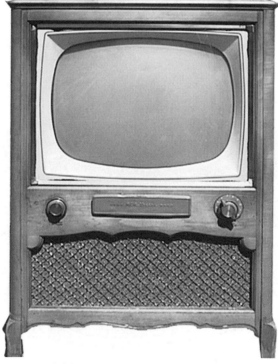

RCA Model 21T Blond Wood Console

RCA Model 5 Prototype Color Console Television from 1953

RCA, Model 5, prototype color console model in dark wood cabinet, 1953, 15"............................... **$10,000**

RCA Model 621TS in Blond Wood Cabinet

RCA, Model 621TS, blond wood tabletop model, 1946, 10" (ILLUS.).. **$2,000**

RCA Model 621TS Table Model in a Dark Wood Cabinet

RCA, Model 621TS, dark wood tabletop, 1946, 7" (ILLUS., top of page) **$1,800**
RCA, Model 630TCS, wooden console model, 1946, 10" **$500**

RCA, Model 630TS, wooden tabletop model, 1946, 10" (ILLUS., bottom of page) **$300**

Early RCA Model 630TS Tabletop Set

RCA Model 641TS

RCA, Model 641TS, wooden console model
w/radio & phonograph, 1947, 10"
(ILLUS., top of page)................................ **$250**
RCA, Model 648PTK, console projection
model w/radio & phonograph, 1947
(ILLUS., next column) **$1,500**
RCA, Model 648PV, wooden projection con-
sole model, 1950.. **$800**

RCA Model 648PTK

RCA Model 6T54 in Tall Metal Cabinet

RCA, Model 6T54, tabletop model in metal cabinet, 1950, 16" (ILLUS.) **$100**

RCA Model 721TS Wooden Tabletop

RCA, Model 721TS, wooden tabletop, 1947, 10" (ILLUS.) **$300**

RCA Model 741PCS Wooden Console Projection Television

RCA, Model 741PCS, wooden console projection model w/wide louvers across the front below the screen, 1948 (ILLUS., top of page) **$1,500**

RCA, Model 741TCS, wooden console model, 1947, 10" **$450**

RCA, Model 8-PT-7010, portable in red metal cabinet, 1956, 8" (ILLUS., bottom of page) **$75**

RCA Model 8-PT-8010 Portable Metal Television

1956 RCA Portable TV in Footed Metal Cabinet

RCA, Model 8-PT-7032, portable in metal cabinet raised on four canted legs, 1956, 8" (ILLUS., top of page) **$75**

RCA, Model 8PCS41, pop-up screen projection model, 1948 .... **$200**

RCA, Model 8T241, wooden tabletop, 1948, 10" (ILLUS., bottom of page) **$150**

RCA Model 8T241

RCA Model 8T244 Wooden Tabletop Set

RCA Model 8T243

RCA, Model 8T243, wooden tabletop, 1948,
10" (ILLUS., to the left) **$150**
RCA, Model 8T244, wooden tabletop model
w/sliding doors, 1948, 10" (ILLUS., top of
page)... **$150-175**
RCA, Model 8T270, wooden tabletop, 1949,
16".. **$125**
RCA, Model 8T271, wooden console model
w/double doors, 1949, 16" **$100**
RCA, Model 8TK29, wooden console model
w/radio, 1949, 10" **$100**
RCA, Model 8TR29, tabletop model w/radio,
1949, 10"... **$175**
RCA, Model 8TS30, wooden tabletop, 1949,
10" (ILLUS., bottom of page) **$175**

RCA Model 8TS30 Wooden Tabletop

RCA Model 8TV41 Wooden Console with Radio & Phonograph

RCA, Model 8TV41, wooden console model w/radio & phonograph, 1949, 10"
(ILLUS.)... **$125**

RCA Model 9PC41 Buffet-style Wooden Console from 1949

RCA, Model 9PC41, wooden buffet-style console projection model, 1949 (ILLUS.).......................... **$250-300**

RCA Model 9T246

RCA, Model 9T240, wooden tabletop, 1949,
10" **$100**
RCA, Model 9T246, tabletop in metal cabi-
net, 1949, 10" (ILLUS., top of page) **$150**
RCA, Model 9T77, wooden console model
w/double doors, 1950, 19" **$75**

RCA, Model 9T89, wooden console model
w/radio & phonograph, 1950, 19" **$75**
RCA, Model CT-100, color console model,
first mass-produced color TV, 1954, 15"
(ILLUS., bottom of page) **$4,000**

RCA Model CT-100 Color Television

RCA Model CTC-10 Color Console Set

RCA, Model CTC-10, color set, console model w/horizontal wood bands across cloth-covered speaker below screen, 1959, 21" (ILLUS., top of page) **$145**

RCA, Model CTC-11, color set, made in tabletop, console or consolette models, 1961, 21", each **$150**

RCA, Model CTC-4, light wood color console model, 1956, 21" (ILLUS., below) **$800**

RCA Model CTC-4 Color Console Set from 1956

RCA Model CTC-5 Color Console TV from 1956

RCA, Model CTC-5, color set, made in tabletop, console or consolette models,
1956, 21", each (ILLUS. of console mod-
el, top of page) **$500**
RCA, Model CTC-7, color console model,
1957, 21" **$300**
RCA, Model CTC-9, color set, made in ta-
bletop, console or consolette models,
1959, 21", each **$250**

RCA, Model T-100, tabletop model in metal
cabinet, 1950, 10" **$100**
RCA, Model T-120, tabletop model in metal
cabinet, 1949, 12" **$75**
RCA, Model T-164, wooden tabletop, 1950,
16" **$75**
RCA, Model TC-165, wooden console mod-
el, 1950, 16" **$50**

Handsome RCA Model TRK-12/120 Console TV with Mirror in the Lid & a Built-in Radio

Rare RCA Model TRK-5 Tall Console

RCA, Model TRK-12/120, console model w/mirror in lid & radio, 1939-40, 12" (ILLUS., bottom previous page) **$8,000**

RCA, Model TRK-5, console model w/radio, 1939, 5" (ILLUS., top of page) **$12,000**

Extremely Rare RCA Model TRK-9/90 Tall Stylish Console TV from 1939-40

Rare RCA Model TT-5 Early Wooden Tabletop TV from 1939

RCA, Model TRK-9/90, tall wooden console model, rounded front corners & raised banding across the bottom front, 1939-40, 9" (ILLUS., bottom previous page) **$15,000**

RCA, Model TT-5, wooden tabletop model w/five-channel tuner, 1939, 5" (ILLUS., top of page) **$12,000**

RCA, Model TV321, wooden console model w/radio, 1949, 10" **$100**

Regal, Model 1007, wooden tabletop, 1948, 10" **$200**

Regal, Model 1207, wooden tabletop, 1948, 12" **$175**

Regal, Model 1208, wooden console model, 1948, 12" **$100**

Regal, Model 1230, tabletop model, 1948, 12" **$175**

Regal, Model 1607, wooden console model, 1949, 16" **$100**

Regal, Model 16T31, wooden tabletop, 1949, 16" **$125**

Regal, Model 16T36, wooden tabletop model w/radio, 1949, 16" **$150**

Rembrandt Model 1950 Table Model with Continuous Tuner

1948 Scott Model 6T11 Projection Set

Rembrandt, Model 1950, wooden tabletop model w/continuous tuner, 1947, 12" (ILLUS., bottom previous page) **$250**

Scott, Model 13A, wooden console w/double doors, 1947, 12" **$800**

Scott, Model 400A, tabletop projection set w/pop-up screen, 1948.............................. **$500**

Scott, Model 6T11, tabletop projection model, 1948 (ILLUS., top of page) **$500**

Scott, Model 800B, wooden projection console model w/radio & phonograph, 1947 .... **$700**

Seiko, Model TR-02-01, television-watch w/radio, 1990, 1" (ILLUS., to the right) **$500**

Sentinal, Model 1201, wooden tabletop, 1950, 12" **$75**

Sentinal, Model 400TV, portable model in a leatherette case, 1948, 7" (ILLUS., top next page) **$200**

Sentinal, Model 401TVM, wooden tabletop, 1948 .... **$150**

Sentinal, Model 402, wooden console model, 1948, 10" **$100**

Sentinal, Model 405, wooden tabletop, 1948, 7" (ILLUS., bottom next page) **$175**

Sentinal, Model 406TVM, wooden tabletop, 1948, 12" **$150**

Seiko 1990 Television-Watch & Radio

Sentinal Model 400 Early Portable TV

Sentinal Model 405

1986 Sharp Model 3-LS-36P Portable

Sentinal, Model 407TVM, wooden console model, 1948, 16" **$100**

Sentinal, Model 412, wooden tabletop, 1949, 10" **$150**

Sentinal, Model 416, wooden console model, 1949, 12" **$100**

Sentinal, Model 419, wooden console model, 1949, 19" **$100**

Sentinal, Model 438, large wooden tabletop set, ca. 1952, 17" **$35**

Sentinal, Model 440, wooden console w/simple lines, 1952, 17" **$35**

Sharp, Model 3-LS36-P, portable model w/hot pink rectangular base & monitor on short pedestal, 1986 (ILLUS., top of page) **$200**

Sharp Model 3-S-111R Portable TV in Red Plastic Case

Sightmaster Model S-15 Wooden Tabletop TV from 1947

Sharp, Model 3-S-111R, portable set in red plastic case, low pedestal base, 1972, 5" (ILLUS., bottom previous page) **$50**

Sightmaster, Model S-15, wooden tabletop, 1947, 15" (ILLUS., top of page) **$250**

Sightmaster, "Sightmirror," wooden tabletop model w/oval mirror flanked by S-scrolls all above a long base drawer, 1948, 15" (ILLUS., bottom of page) **$350**

Silvertone (Sears), Model 101, wooden tabletop, 1949, 12" **$175**

Silvertone (Sears), Model 101A, wooden console model w/radio & phonograph, double doors, 1949, 12" **$100**

Silvertone (Sears), Model 112, wooden tabletop, 1949, 12" **$150**

Silvertone (Sears), Model 125, tabletop model, 1949, 10" **$175**

Silvertone (Sears), Model 132, blond wood tabletop model, 1949, 12" **$175**

Silvertone (Sears), Model 133, wooden tabletop, 1949, 12" **$150**

Silvertone (Sears), Model 3132, wooden tabletop model w/pushbutton tuning, 1949, 10" **$225**

Silvertone (Sears), Model 8130, wooden tabletop, 1949, 7" **$200**

Silvertone (Sears), Model 8133, wooden tabletop model w/pushbutton tuning, 1949, 10" **$225**

Silvertone (Sears), Model 9111, wooden tabletop, 1949, 10" **$175**

Unusual & Elegant Sightmaster "Sightmirror" Table Television

Sinclair Model FTV1 LCD Television

Silvertone (Sears), Model 9112, wooden tabletop, 1949, 12" **$150**

Silvertone (Sears), Model 9113, wooden tabletop, 1949, 10" **$175**

Silvertone (Sears), Model 9114, wooden tabletop, 1949, 12" **$150**

Silvertone (Sears), Model 9115, portable model w/leatherette case, 1949, 8" **$250**

Silvertone (Sears), Model 9116, portable model in leatherette case, 1949, 7" **$250**

Silvertone (Sears), Model 9120, wooden tabletop, 1949, 12" **$150**

Silvertone (Sears), Model 9121, wooden tabletop model w/double doors & push-button tuning, 1949, 12" **$200**

Silvertone (Sears), Model 9122, wooden console model w/pushbutton tuning & double doors, 1949, 12" **$200**

Silvertone (Sears), Model 9125, tabletop model in Bakelite cabinet, 1949, 10" **$150**

Silvertone (Sears), Model 9127, wooden console model, 1949, 12" **$100**

Silvertone (Sears), Model 9128, blond wood console model w/pushbutton tuning & double doors, 1949, 12" **$125**

Silvertone (Sears), Model 9130, wooden console model, 1949, 12" **$100**

Silvertone (Sears), Model 9133, wooden console model w/pull-out phonograph, 1949, 10" **$100**

Sinclair, Model FTV1, small LCD, 1981, 2 1/2" (ILLUS., top of page) **$50**

Sinclair Model MTV-1 Small Rectangular Portable

Sinclair, Model MTV-1, small rectangular portable w/built-in antenna, 1979, 1 3/4" (ILLUS., top of page)............................ **$200-300**

Sinclair, Model MTV1B, small set in plastic case, made for the British market, 1978, 1 3/4" (ILLUS., bottom of page) **$150**

Sinclair Model MTV1B Made for the British Market

Snaider "Auditorium" Projection Set

Snaider, Model P521, "Auditorium," projection console model in a metal cabinet, 1948 (ILLUS., top of page)........................ **$500**

Sony, Model 5-303, portable model in a plastic cabinet, 1965, 5"............................. **$75**

Sony Model 8-301W 1961 Portable Set

Sony Model FDM-330 LCD TV

Sony, Model 8-301W, oblong transistor portable w/metal cabinet, 1961, 8" (ILLUS.,
bottom previous page) **$250-300**
Sony, Model BP-6, portable set in a plastic
cabinet, 1965, 3 1/2" **$100**
Sony, Model FD-10, LCD in plastic cabinet,
1989, 2" **$80**
Sony, Model FD-210, "Watchman" model in
plastic case, 1988, 1 3/4" **$200**
Sony, Model FD-40, "Watchman" model in
plastic case, 1989, 2" **$75**
Sony, Model FDL-310, "Watchman" model
in plastic case, 1988, 2 1/2" **$180**

Sony, Model FDL-3500, color portable set,
1989, 3" **$300**
Sony, Model FDM-330, LCD television that
snaps together (ILLUS., top of page) **$200**
Sony, Model KV-4100, portable color set,
1981, 3 1/2" (ILLUS., bottom of page)
.... **$500**
Sony, Model TV-900U, "Sony the Giant,"
black & white portable, 1960s, 8" **$25**
Sparton, Model 24TR10, wooden console
w/a large gold mask around the screen,
1950, 12" **$45**

Sony Model KV-4100 Portable Color Television

Sparton Model 4900 Console Model with Mirrored Lid & Radio & Phonograph

Sparton, Model 4900, console model w/mirror in lid & radio & phonograph, 1949, 10" (ILLUS.)... **$450**

Sparton, Model 4900TV, wooden console w/mirror in the lid & a radio & phonograph, 1948, 10"....................................... **$125**

Sparton, Model 4901, blond wood console model w/mirror in lid, 1949, 12"................. **$450**

Sparton, Model 4916, wooden console model w/radio & phonograph, 1949, 10"
.... **$100**

Sparton, Model 4917, wooden console model w/radio & phonograph, 1949, 10"
.... **$100**

Sparton, Model 4918, blond wood console model w/radio & phonograph, 1949, 10"
.... **$125**

Sparton, Model 4920, wooden console model w/double doors, 1949, 12" **$100**

Sparton, Model 4939, wooden console model w/mirror in lid & radio, 1949, 12"
.... **$400**

Sparton Model 4940 Large 1949 Console

Sparton, Model 4940, wooden console model w/mirror in lid & radio, 1949, 10" **$400**

Sparton, Model 4940, wooden console model w/mirror in the lid, large speaker in the lower front, 1949, 12" (ILLUS., top of page) **$400**

Sparton, Model 4941, blond wood console model w/mirror in lid & radio, 1949, 10" **$500**

Sparton, Model 4951, wooden tabletop, 1949, 12" (ILLUS., top of next page) **$125**

Sparton, Model 4951, wooden tabletop model w/small speakers flanking the screen, 1949, 10" **$150**

Sparton, Model 4952, blond wood tabletop, 1949, 10" **$150**

Sparton, Model 4954, wooden tabletop, 1949, 10" **$150**

Sparton, Model 4960, wooden tabletop, 1949, 12" **$125**

Sparton, Model 4964, wooden console model w/double doors, 1949, 16" **$75**

Sparton, Model 5002, wooden tabletop, 1950, 10" **$125**

Sparton, Model 5006, wooden tabletop, 1950, 10" **$125**

Sparton, Model 5010 or 5014, tabletop model w/painted glass faceplate, each **$65**

Sparton, Model 5057, tall blond wood console model w/large speaker in the lower front, 1949, 12" (ILLUS., bottom of next page) **$75**

Stewart Warner, Model 9054, wooden console model w/mirror in the lid, 1948, 10" **$500**

Sparton Model 4951

Stewart Warner, Model 9100A, wooden tabletop model w/pushbutton tuning, 1949,
12" **$300**

Stewart Warner, Model 9100B, wooden
console model w/mirror in the lid, 1949,
10" **$500**

Tall Sparton Console TV from 1949

Stromberg Carlson Unique Chinese Classic Console Television

Stewart Warner, Model 9120A, wooden tabletop, 1950, 16" **$75**

Stewart Warner, Model 9120B, wooden console model, 1950, 16" **$50**

Stewart Warner, Model 9120E, blond wood console model w/double doors, 1950, 16" **$75**

Stewart Warner, Model T-711, wooden console model w/radio, 1948, 10" **$200**

Stromberg Carlson, Chinese Classic hand-painted console model, red w/black borders & gold Chinese figural center panels & scattered floral designs, 1954, 21" (ILLUS., top of page) **$200**

Stromberg Carlson, Model 24RP, wooden console model w/radio & phonograph, 1951, 24" (ILLUS., bottom of page) **$200**

Stromberg Carlson Model 24RP Console TV with Radio & Phonograph

Stromberg Carlson Model TC-10 Wooden Tabletop with Continuous Tuning

Stromberg Carlson, Model TC-10, wooden tabletop w/continuous tuning, 1949, 10" (ILLUS., top of page).................................. **$400**

Stromberg Carlson, Model TC-125HM, wooden tabletop, 1949, 12" **$150**

Stromberg Carlson, Model TC-125LA, wooden console model, 1949, 12" **$100**

Stromberg Carlson, Model TC-19, wooden console model, 1949, 19".......................... **$100**

Stromberg Carlson, Model TS-125, wooden console model w/radio, 1949, 12" **$100**

Stromberg Carlson, Model TS-16, wooden console model w/radio & phonograph, 1949, 15" **$100**

Stromberg Carlson, Model TV-10L, wooden tabletop model w/pushbutton tuning, 1947, 10"... **$500**

Stromberg Carlson, Model TV-10P, wooden console model w/pushbutton tuning, 1947, 10"... **$400**

Stromberg Carlson, Model TV-12H2, wooden tabletop, 1947, 12" **$300**

Stromberg Carlson, Model TV-12LM, wooden console model w/double doors, 1947, 12" (ILLUS., bottom of page) **$300**

Stromberg Carlson Model TV-12LM Set

Stromberg Carlson Model TX-18LX Console with Phonograph Attachment

Stromberg Carlson, Model TX-18LX, wooden console model w/45 rpm phonograph attachment, 1949, 20"
(ILLUS.)... **$200**

Stromberg Carlson 1950s Blond Wood Console

Stromberg Carlson, Model X21, blond wood console model on four pointed legs, 1950s, 21" (ILLUS.)
.... **$75**

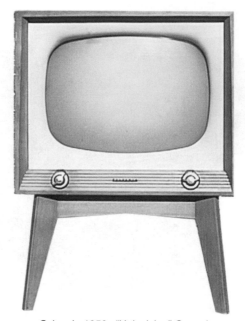

Sylvania 1950s "Halovision" Console

Sylvania, "Halovision" console in a blond wood cabinet raised on tall tapering legs, 1950s (ILLUS., top of page) **$225**

Sylvania, Model 120B, "Halolight," blond wood tabletop model, 1952, 21" **$200**

Sylvania, Model 120M, "Halolight," wooden tabletop, 1952, 21" **$200**

Sylvania, Model 172, "Halolight," wooden console model, 1952, 21" **$200**

Sylvania, Model 21C405, "Halolight," wooden console model, 1959, 21" **$150**

Sylvania, Model 21C529, "Halolight," wooden consolette model, 1959, 21" **$150**

Sylvania, Model 21T305, "Halolight," wooden tabletop, 1959, 21" **$150**

Sylvania Model 526m "Halolight" Set

Teco Wooden Tabletop TV with Large Porthole Screen

Sylvania, Model 526m "Halolight," dark wood console model, white light around the screen, 1959, 21" (ILLUS., bottom previous page) **$225**

Teco, wooden tabletop model w/large porthole screen & curved end speakers, 1948, 10" (ILLUS., top of page) **$300**

Tele-King, Model 210, wooden tabletop model, 1948, 10" **$200**

Tele-King, Model 310, wooden console model, 1948, 10" **$100**

Tele-King, Model 410, wooden tabletop model, 1949, 10" **$200**

Tele-King, Model 512, wooden tabletop model, 1949, 12" **$200**

Tele-King, Model 612, wooden console model, 1949, 12" **$100**

Tele-King, Model 616, wooden tabletop model, 1949, 16" **$125**

Tele-King, Model 710, wooden console model, 1949, 10" **$100**

Tele-King, Model C-816, wooden console model, 1949, 16" **$100**

Tele-King, Model T-510, wooden tabletop model, 1949, 10" **$150**

Tele-King, Model T-712, wooden tabletop model, 1949, 12" **$125**

Teletone, Model TV-149, wooden tabletop, 1948, 7" (ILLUS., bottom of page) **$150-225**

Teletone, Model TV-208, cloth-covered portable model, 1948, 7" **$175**

Teletone, Model TV-209, wooden tabletop, 1949, 10" **$150**

Teletone Model TV-149 Tabletop Set

Teletone Cloth-covered Portable TV from 1948

Teletone, Model TV-220, cloth-covered portable model w/hinged cover, 1948, 7" (ILLUS., top of page).................................. **$175**

Teletone, Model TV-249, wooden tabletop, 1949, 10".. **$150**

Teletone, Model TV-250, tabletop model in Bakelite cabinet, 1949, 10" **$175**

Teletone, Model TV-254, tabletop model in Bakelite cabinet, 1949, 10" **$175**

Teletone, Model TV-255, tabletop model in Bakelite cabinet, 1949, 10" **$175**

Teletone, Model TV-256, tabletop model in Bakelite cabinet, 1949, 10" **$125**

Teletone, Model TV-279, wooden console model, 1949, 10".. **$125**

Teletone, Model TV-282, wooden console model w/double doors, 1949, 10" **$125**

Teletone, Model TV-285, wooden tabletop, 1950, 16".. **$125**

Teletone, Model TV-300, tabletop model in Bakelite cabinet, 1950, 10" **$150**

Templetone Model TV-1776 Wooden Tabletop 1948 Television

Transvision Kit TV with Wooden Front Panel

Templetone Mfg. Co., Model TV-1776, wooden tabletop model w/magnifying lens, 1948, 7" (ILLUS., bottom previous page) **$1,200**

Transvision, kit TV in factory cabinet, 1946, 7" (ILLUS., top of page) **$2,000**
Transvision, kit TV in Tele-Kit cabinet, 1946, 7" (ILLUS., bottom of page) **$2,000**

Early Transvision Kit TV from 1946

Transvision Kit TV in Tele-kit Cabinet Variation

Transvision Kit TV Set in Factory Cabinet

Transvision, kit TV in Tele-Kit cabinet variation, 1946, 7" (ILLUS., top of page)....... **$2,000**
Transvision, kit TV w/wooden front panel, 1946, 7" (ILLUS., second from top)......... **$1,500**
Transvision, Model 10A, kit TV w/wooden cabinet, 1947, 10" **$800**
Transvision, Model 10BL, wooden tabletop model w/built-in magnifier, 1947, 10" **$1,500**
Transvision, Model 10CL, wooden tabletop model w/built-in magnifier, 1947, 10" **$1,500**

Transvision, Model 12BL, wooden tabletop, 1947, 12".. **$250**
Transvision, Model 7BL, wooden tabletop model w/five-channel tuner & built-in magnifier, 1947, 7"................................ **$2,000**
Transvision, Model 7CL, wooden tabletop, 1947, 7".. **$1,500**
Transvision, Model 7FL, wooden tabletop, 1947, 7".. **$1,500**

Transvision Model A Kit TV in Cabinet

Transvision, Model A, kit TV in factory cabinet, 1948, 12" (ILLUS., top of page).......... **$500**

Truetone (Western Auto), Model D-1090, wooden console model, 1949, 16" **$75**

Truetone (Western Auto), Model D-1990, wooden tabletop, 1949, 10" **$150**

Truetone (Western Auto), Model D-1991, wooden console model, 1949, 10" **$100**

Truetone (Western Auto), Model D-1992, porthole wooden console w/radio & phonograph, two large doors decorated w/raised panels above cloth-covered speaker panels, 1949, 10" (ILLUS. closed, bottom of page)............................ **$250**

Truetone (Western Auto), Model D-1998, wooden console model, 1949, 12" **$100**

Truetone (Western Auto), Model D-2044, wooden tabletop, 1949, 10" **$150**

Truetone (Western Auto), Model D-2050, wooden tabletop, 1949, 10" **$150**

Truetone (Western Auto), Model D-2985, wooden tabletop, 1949, 7" **$200**

United States Television, Model KRV-12831, wooden console model w/radio & phonograph, 1948, 12" **$125**

United States Television, Model KRV-15381, wooden console model w/radio & phonograph, 1948, 15" **$100**

United States Television, Model T-10823, wooden tabletop, 1949, 10" **$150**

United States Television, Model T-15823, wooden tabletop, 1949, 10" **$150**

United States Television, Model T-502, wooden console model w/radio & phonograph & double doors, 1949, 10" **$125**

United States Television, Model T-507, wooden projection console model w/radio & phonograph, 1949............................ **$250**

United States Television, Model T-508, projection console model w/radio & phonograph in a leatherette cabinet, 1949 ...... **$300**

Truetone Model D1992 Shown Closed

United States Television Model T-525

United States Television, Model T-525, wooden projection console model, 1949 (ILLUS., top of page) **$250**
United States Television, Model T-530, wooden projection console model, 1949
.... **$250**
United States Television, Model T-621, wooden projection console model, 1949
.... **$250**

Videodyne, Model 10-FM, wooden tabletop model w/radio, 1948, 10" (ILLUS., bottom of page) **$1,800**
Videodyne, Model 10-TV, wooden tabletop, 1948, 10" **$2,000**
Videodyne, Model 12-FM, wooden tabletop model w/radio, 1948, 12" **$1,500**
Videodyne, Model 12-TV, wooden tabletop, 1948, 12" **$1,500**

Videodyne Model 10-FM Early Table Model TV Set

Unusual Viewtone Model VP-100 Table Model Television

Viewtone, Model VP-100 "Futura," tabletop
model, 1946, 7" (ILLUS., top of page) **$2,000**
Viewtone, Model VP-101, wooden console
model w/radio & six-channel tuner, 1946,
7" **$3,000**

Viewtone, Model VP-102, wooden console
model w/radio & phonograph, 1946, 7"
.... **$3,000**
Western Television, Visionette mechanical
TV set, 1931 (ILLUS., below)................ **$8,000**

Rare Very Early Western Television "Visionette" Mechanical TV from 1931

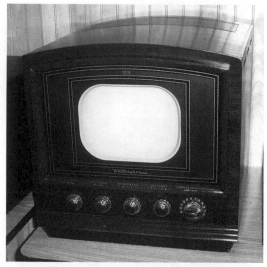

Westinghouse Model H-196 Tabletop TV Set from 1949

Westinghouse, Model H-181, wooden console model w/double doors, 1949, 10" **$100**

Westinghouse, Model H-196, wooden tabletop w/arched cabinet, 1949, 12" (ILLUS., top of page) **$200**

Westinghouse, Model H-207, wooden console model w/radio & phonograph, 1949, 10" **$100**

Westinghouse, Model H-216, wooden console model w/lift-up screen, 1949, 16" **$250**

Westinghouse, Model H-217, wooden console model w/radio & phonograph, 1949, 12" **$100**

Westinghouse, Model H-223, wooden tabletop, 1949, 10" **$150**

Westinghouse, Model H-226, wooden console model w/double doors, 1949, 12" **$100**

Westinghouse, Model H-231, blond wood console model w/radio & phonograph, 1949, 10" **$125**

Westinghouse, Model H-242, wooden tabletop, 1948, 12" **$175**

Westinghouse, Model H-251, wooden tabletop, 1948, 12" **$175**

Westinghouse, Model H-600T16, wooden tabletop, 1948, 16" **$150**

Westinghouse, Model H-601K12, wooden console model, 1948, 12" **$125**

Westinghouse, Model H-602K12, wooden console model, 1948, 12" **$125**

Westinghouse Model H-609T10 Wooden Tabletop Set from 1948

Westinghouse Model H840CK15 Color Console Set from 1954

Westinghouse, Model H-604T10, wooden tabletop, 1948, 10" **$200**

Westinghouse, Model H-605T12, wooden tabletop, 1948, 12" **$175**

Westinghouse, Model H-608K10, wooden console model, 1948, 10" **$125**

Westinghouse, Model H-609T10, wooden tabletop, 1948, 10" (ILLUS., bottom of previous page) **$200**

Westinghouse, Model H-626T16, wooden tabletop, 1950, 16" **$100**

Westinghouse, Model H-627K16, wooden console model, 1950, 16" **$75**

Westinghouse, Model H-629K16, wooden console model, 1950, 16" **$75**

Westinghouse, Model H-840CK15, wooden color console model w/a pair of large doors, 1954, 15" (ILLUS., top of page) ... **$5,000**

Westinghouse, Model WRT-700, wooden tabletop model w/a stepped top & panels of nice veneering, (labeled RCA), 1939, 5" (ILLUS., bottom of page) **$12,000**

Very Rare Westinghouse Model WRT-700 Wooden Tabletop Set

Early & Very Rare Westinghouse Model WRT-701 Console Set in Art Deco Cabinet

Westinghouse, Model WRT-701, wooden console model w/radio in Art Deco style fancy cabinet, (labeled RCA), 1939, 5" (ILLUS.)... **$15,000**

One of the Rarest Console TVs - Westinghouse Model WRT-702

Westinghouse, Model WRT-702, wooden console model w/radio (labeled RCA), 1939, 9" (ILLUS.)
.... **$15,000**

Early Westinghouse Model WRT-703 Console

Westinghouse, Model WRT-703 (aka Model TRK-12), wooden console model w/mirror in lid & radio (labeled RCA), 1939, 12" (ILLUS.).. **$12,000**

Zenith Blond Wood 1950s Console TV

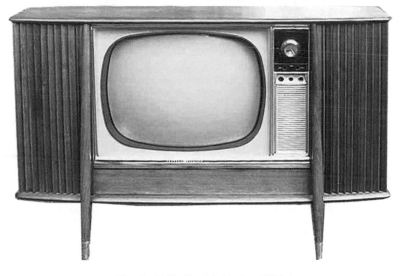

Classic 1960s Danish Modern TV Set

Zenith, console in a blond wood cabinet raised on four pointed legs, mid-1950s (ILLUS., top of page).................................. **$100**

Zenith, Danish Modern fine wood cabinet console model on slender pointed legs, 1960s (ILLUS., middle of page) **$225**

Zenith, Model 24G20-G2420R, "Newport," mahogany tabletop model w/porthole screen, 1950 .... **$75**

Zenith, Model 24G21-G2454R, mahogany console model w/porthole screen, 1950 ...... **$95**

Zenith, Model 27T965, porthole wooden console model, 1948, 12" **$300**

Zenith, Model 28T925E, porthole blond wood tabletop model, 1949, 10" **$400**

Zenith, Model 28T925R, wooden porthole tabletop model, 1949, 10" **$350**

Zenith, Model 28T926, wooden porthole screen model, 1949, 16" **$350**

Zenith Model G2340

Zenith, Model 28T960E, blond wood port-
hole console, 1949, 12".............................. **$350**
Zenith, Model 28T960E, blond wood port-
hole console model, 1949, 12".................. **$350**
Zenith, Model 28T960K, wooden porthole
console model, 1949, 12".......................... **$325**
Zenith, Model 28T961E, blond wood port-
hole console model, 1949, 10".................. **$350**
Zenith, Model 28T962R, wooden porthole
console model, 1949, 12".......................... **$325**
Zenith, Model 28T963R, blond wood port-
hole console model, 1949, 10".................. **$350**
Zenith, Model 3267, wooden porthole console model w/radio & phonograph, 1951,
16"... **$200**
Zenith, Model 37T996, wooden porthole
console model w/radio & phonograph,
1949, 16"... **$250**
Zenith, Model 42T999E, wooden porthole
console model w/radio & phonograph,
1949, 16"... **$250**
Zenith, Model A1512, portable model in
metal cabinet, 1956, 16" **$60**
Zenith, Model G2322, tabletop w/porthole
Bakelite or wooden cabinet, 1950, 12"....... **$300**
Zenith, Model G2327, wooden porthole tabletop model, 1950, 12" **$300**
Zenith, Model G2327R7, porthole tabletop
model in leatherette cabinet, 1950, 12"
.... **$250**

Zenith, Model G2340, wooden porthole
console model, 1950, 12" (ILLUS., top of
page)... **$250**
Zenith, Model G2350, wooden porthole
console model, 1950, 12" **$250**
Zenith, Model G2353, wooden porthole
console model, 1950, 12" **$250**
Zenith, Model G2353E, blond wood port-
hole console model, 1950, 12".................. **$275**
Zenith, Model G2355, blond wood porthole
console model, 1950, 12" **$275**
Zenith, Model G2356, wooden porthole
console model, 1950, 12" **$250**
Zenith, Model G2420E, blond wood port-
hole tabletop model, 1950, 12" **$300**
Zenith, Model G2420R, wooden porthole
tabletop model, 1950, 12" **$275**
Zenith, Model G2437, wooden porthole
console model, 1950, 16" **$250**
Zenith, Model G2437EZ, blond wood port-
hole console model w/double doors,
1950, 16".. **$225**
Zenith, Model G2437RZ, wooden porthole
console model w/double doors, 1950, 16" .. **$225**
Zenith, Model G2441, wooden porthole
console model, 1950, 16" **$250**
Zenith, Model G2442E, blond wooden port-
hole console model, 1950, 16".................. **$275**
Zenith, Model G2442R, wooden porthole
console model, 1950, 16" **$250**

1951 Zenith Console with Porthole Screen

Zenith, Model G2448, wooden porthole console model, 1950, 16".......................... **$250**

Zenith, Model G2845, wooden porthole console model, 1950, 12".......................... **$250**

Zenith, Model G2951, wooden porthole console model, 1950, 16".......................... **$250**

Zenith, Model G2952, wooden porthole console model, 1950, 16".......................... **$250**

Zenith, Model G2957, wooden porthole console model w/radio & phonograph, 1950, 12"... **$250**

Zenith, Model G2958, wooden porthole console model w/radio & phonograph, 1950, 12"... **$250**

Zenith, Model G3059, wooden porthole console model w/radio & phonograph, 1950, 16"... **$250**

Zenith, Model G3062, wooden porthole console model w/radio & phonograph, 1950, 16"... **$250**

Zenith, Model G3173, wooden porthole console model w/radio & phonograph, 1950, 16"... **$250**

Zenith, Model G3275, wooden porthole console model w/radio & phonograph, 1950, 16"... **$250**

Zenith, Model H2226E, blond wood porthole tabletop model, 1951, 12"................. **$225**

Zenith, Model H2226R, wooden porthole tabletop model, 1951, 12".......................... **$200**

Zenith, Model H2437E, wooden porthole console model, 1951, 16".......................... **$200**

Zenith, Model H2438, wooden porthole console model, 1951, 16".......................... **$200**

Zenith, Model H2445, wooden porthole console model, 1951, 19".......................... **$200**

Zenith, Model H2447, wooden porthole console model, 1951, 19".......................... **$200**

Zenith, Model H2449E, wooden porthole console model, 1951, 16" (ILLUS., top of page).. **$200**

Zenith, Model H3267, wooden console model w/porthole screen & radio & phonograph, 1951, 16"...................................... **$200**

Zenith, Model H3269E, blond wood console model w/porthole screen & radio & phonograph, 1951, 16"................................... **$225**

Zenith, Model H3469E, blond wood porthole console model w/radio & phonograph, 1951, 16"...................................... **$225**

Zenith, Model H3477, wooden porthole console model w/radio & phonograph, 1951, 19"... **$200**

Zenith Console with ""Band Shell" Speaker

Zenith, Model R1912R7, metal & wood console cabinet w/"band shell" speaker, 1954 (ILLUS.)............. **$150**

1970s Modernistic Zenith TV

Zenith, Model SF-1964X, white plastic Modernistic pedestal-base cabinet, 1975 (ILLUS.) **$145**

Original Advertisements

A colorful magazine ad featuring a variety of Sentinel radios.
335-PI, 335-PW, 335-PG, & 335-M.

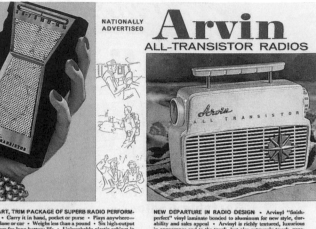
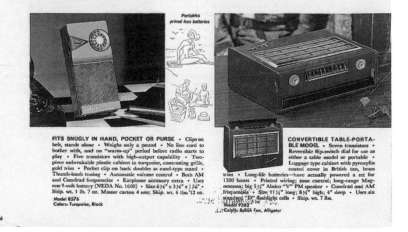
Arvin All-Transistor Radios Ad.

Philco All-American Portable All Transistor Radios for 1960.

The Incomparable Capehart "Rhapsody II" Television Ad.

MODEL TC-62 (SAGE GREEN)

THE INCOMPARABLE

Capehart

"De luxe 6" CLOCK RADIO

Presenting a brand-new Clock Radio by Capehart, the recognized style
leader—the Capehart "Deluxe 6" Clock Radio. Greater range and sensitivity
provide reception and tone to rival the finest console instrument. Five
smart decorator colors. An 1100 watt appliance outlet makes the
"Deluxe 6" an invaluable household servant, too. The Capehart "Deluxe 6"
is rightly called the World's Most Beautiful Clock Radio.

MODEL TC-62 (IVORY)

MODEL TC-62 (GRAY-BLUE)

MODEL TC-62 (BURGUNDY)

MODEL TC-62 (EBONY)

The Incomparable Capehart "Deluxe 6" Clock Radio

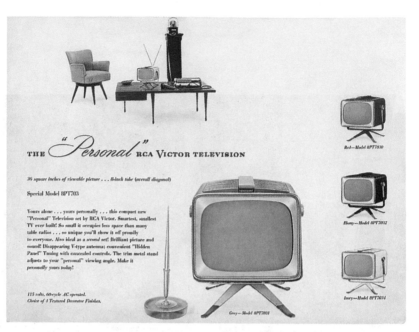

The "Personal" RCA Victor Television

The "Ranstead" RCA Victor Television

Motorola *Model 52R*

A triumph of compact design and beautiful styling! Here's a small radio that gives big Golden Voice performance yet is exceptionally light and easy to move about the home. Big radio features including new magnetic core antenna for best reception.

AVAILABLE IN 6 DECORATOR COLORS:
52R11, Walnut • 52R12, Ivory • 52R13, Maroon
52R14, Gray • 52R15, Forest Green • 52R16, Red

Motorola Model 52R Radio

Muntz Televisions, The Vagabond, The Holiday, The Utility,
The Westfield, The Claridge, The Sheridan and The Wedgwood.

The incomparable Muntz, "The Capri" 21-Inch TV-Radio-Phonograph Stereo

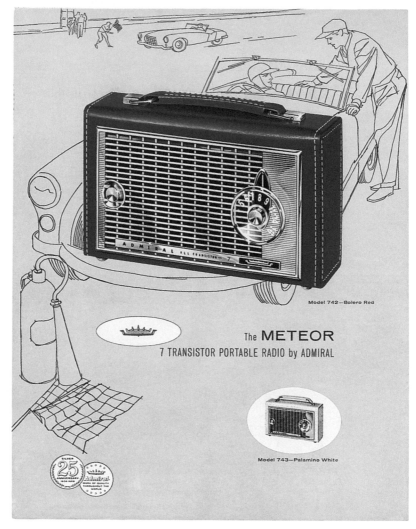

The Meteor 7 Transistor Portable Radio by Admiral.

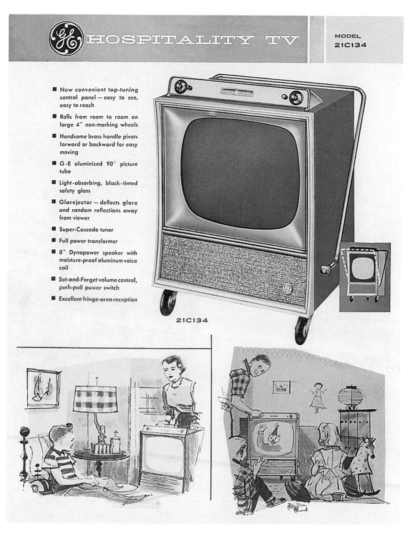

GE Hospitality TV, Model 21C134.

Philco "Predicta" Television, Models 4710 & 4710-L.

4686-S
Genuine stripe mahogany
4686-SL
Genuine white blond oak
4686-SR
Mahogany with remote control
4686-SLR
White oak with remote control

PHILCO *Mastercraft* COLLECTION

THE *Miss America 21*

Directa WIRELESS REMOTE CONTROL

- Dramatic New Swivel Console with Brass-Tipped Feet
- Directa Electrostatic Remote Control on "R" Models
- Exclusive Wrap-Around 3-Speaker Wide Diffusion Sound System
- Top Tuning
- New Pre-Set Fine Tuning
- HI-Voltage 10L60 Chassis

- Illuminated Pop-up on-off Switch and Channel Selection
- Transformer Powered
- Deluxe Cascode Tuner
- 110° Aluminized SF Picture Tube
- New Higher Fidelity Audio Power System
- Full Range Variable Tone Control
- Positive Picture Lock

- 3-Position Electronic Range Switch
- Built-in UHF-VHF Antenna
- Front Removable Filter Glass
- All Channel UHF on "U" Model
- Perma-Circuit Chassis Construction with all components and circuits identified for ease of service
- Underwriters' Approved
- 117 Volts, 60 Cycle AC

33¹¹/₁₆" high, 28½" wide, 13¹¹/₃₂" deep, 21-inch overall diagonal measurement, 262 square inch viewable area

Philco "Mastercraft" Collection ad featuring The Miss America 21 Model

The Sylvania Prospector AC/DC-Battery Portable Radio. Model 3401.

Sylvania Star Timer Super Deluxe Clock-Radio. Model 2301.

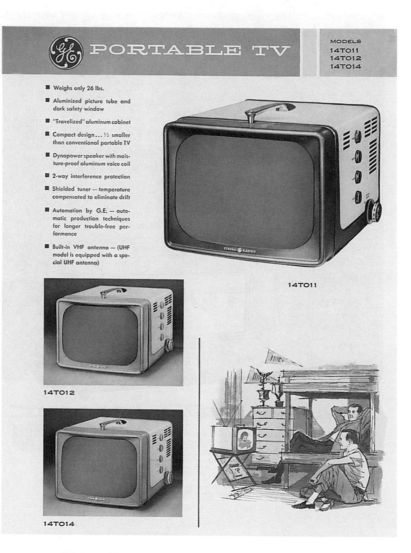

GE Portable TV, Models 14TO11, 14TO12, 14TO14.

The Wickford, a Contemporary Console Model by DuMont, 1950s

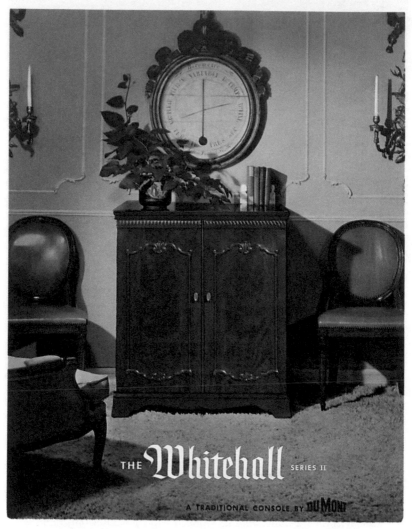

The Whitehall Series II, a Traditional Console TV by DuMont.

Admiral Giant 21" TV-Radio-Phonograph

Admiral Giant 21" TV Console.

Crosley Automatic Television.

the **MOTOROLA** transistor **POCKET RADIO**

MODEL 56T

the 56T1 . . . in Antique White with Vertical Plano Rotating Antenna handle in Antique White. (Shown Actual Size)

Also available in:
Chrome and Ebony—56T2.

No more stunning pocket radio in all the world. Up to 3 times more power than other pocket portables. Electronic miracle . . . transistors . . . supply this amazing power! The *only* pocket radio with a Rotating Antenna handle *and* an unbreakable metal case.

The Motorola Transistor Pocket Radio, Model 56T.

Humidity-Proof...for protection against radio's greatest enemy !

New Zenith's Special "Tropic Treatment"

GUARANTEES Perfect Performance

Even Under the Worst of Humid Conditions!

Every sportsman knows how humidity ruts and rusts equipment. Humidity is radio's greatest enemy, too. But when you take this new Zenith *humidity-proof* portable on your trips, you enjoy perfect performance where other radios fail.

In swamp, ravine, boat, tropical climate—any-

where, this Zenith Trans-Oceanic pulls in standard broadcast coast to coast, plus world-wide short wave on 5 international bands—Just press a button and tune 'em in! Plays in trains, planes, boats, cars, steel buildings, remote areas. Made possible by Zenith's exclusive Wavemagnets (U.S. Patents 2164251 ... 2200674). Styled like finest luggage. Works on battery pack (up to a year's normal use) and on AC or DC current. No wonder it's top choice of America's sportsmen. See and hear it at your radio dealer's today!

Model 8G005Y   **$114.40***

* Slightly extra. West Coast price slightly higher.

NEW Zenith TRANS-OCEANIC PORTABLE

RADIO Zenith Radio Corp., Chicago 39, Illinois

Copr. 1947, Zenith Radio Corporation

Ad for the Zenith Trans-Oceanic Portable Radio

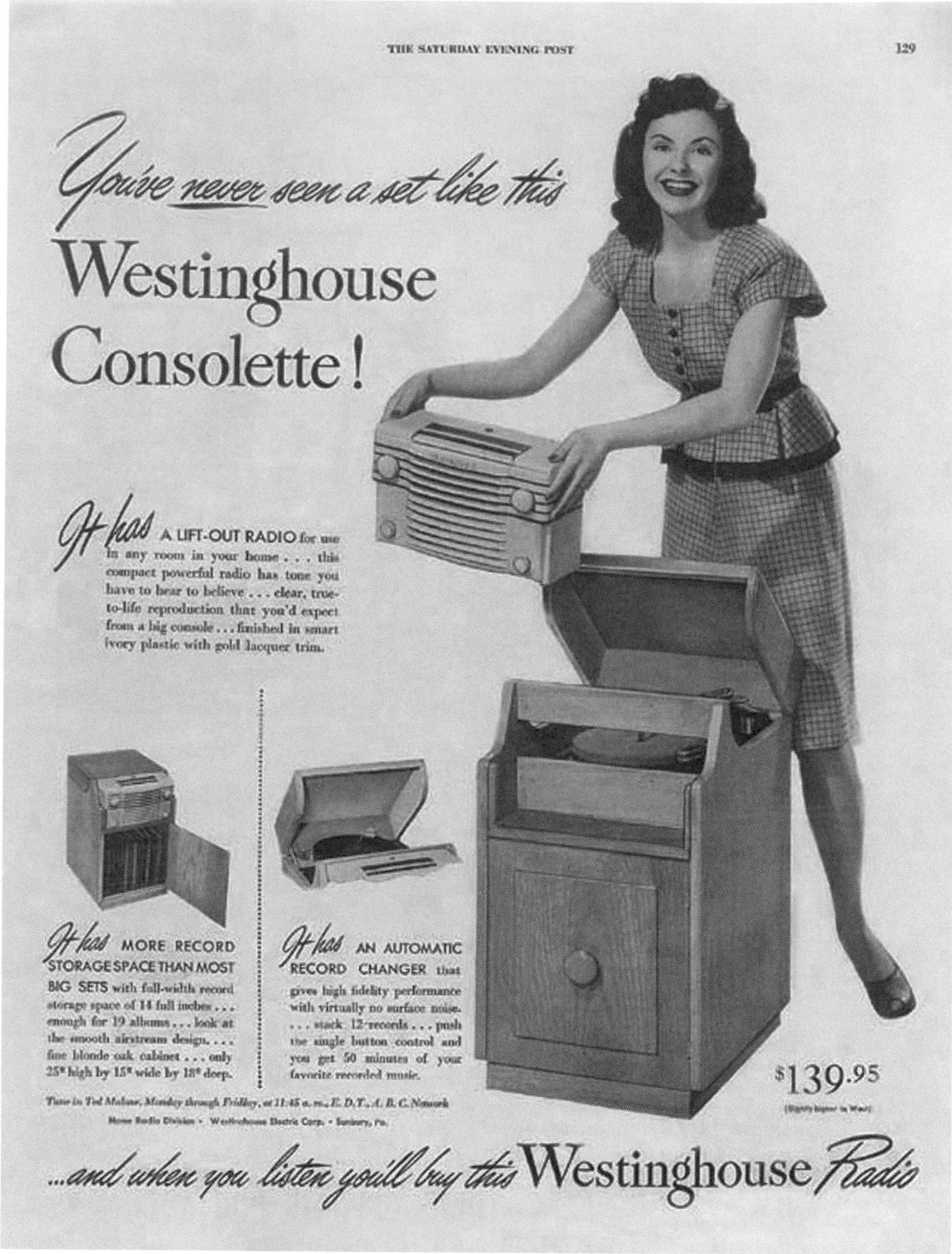

Westinghouse Consolette.

Truetone 1938 Radio Log.

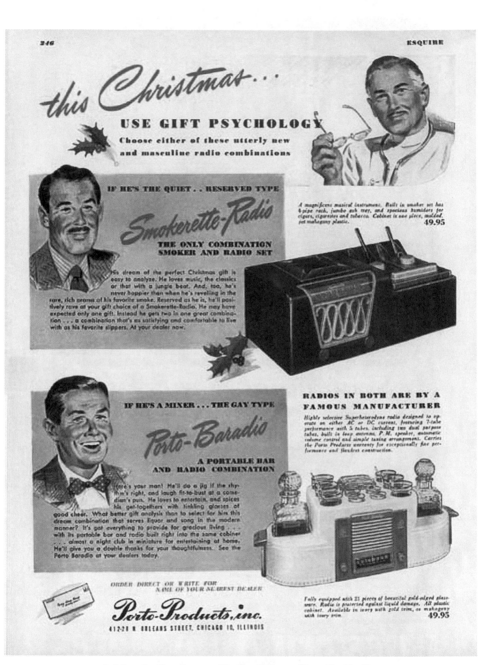

Ad for the Smokerette-Radio & Porto-Baradio Radios

Special Feature

Zenith Model H615 portable w/top handle, Bakelite, 1951, **$25-50**

Westinghouse Model H17TS radios ca. 1950s, each **$50-75**

Universal radio with 'cathedral' style cabinet, ca. 1931, **$75-100**

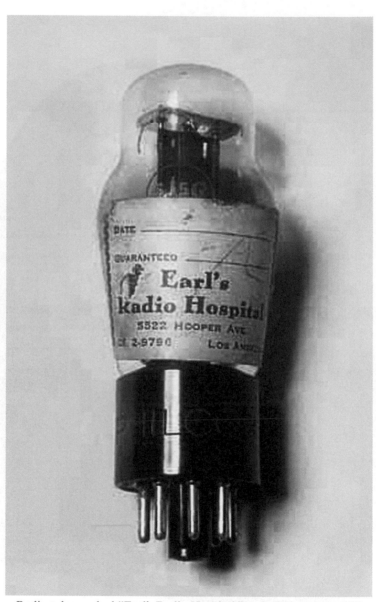

Radio tube marked "Earl's Radio Hospital," early 20th century, **$25**

Stewart Warner "Minerva" model, Model R-1866, 1937, **$150-200**

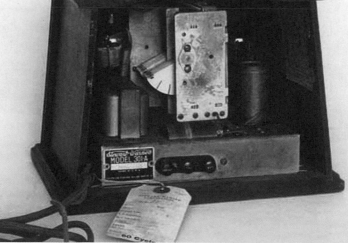

Stewart Warner Model 301A with short-wave, front & back views, 1930, **$50-75**

Stewart Warner Model R-180, side table-style wood cabinet with shelves, 1937, **$50-75**

Silvertone Model 1600 radio with short-wave - front & back views, 1933, **$75-100**

Silvertone Model 4569, 1937, **$150-200**

Silvertone Model 1711A (stepped Art Deco-style cabinet), World's Fair model, 1933, **$150-200**

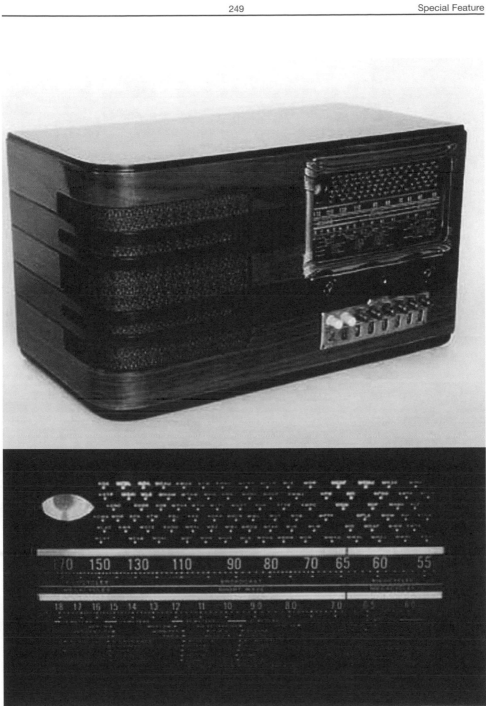

RPC Model 7G radio - front & back views, 1938, **$75-100**

Reela 2 radio, French - front & back views, ca. 1950, **$75-100**

Pilot Model FM607 radio, ca. 1950, **$50-75**

Pilot Model T601 radio in dark wood case, ca. 1950, **$25-50**

Philips Model BD290U radio, front & back view, 1950, **$50-75**

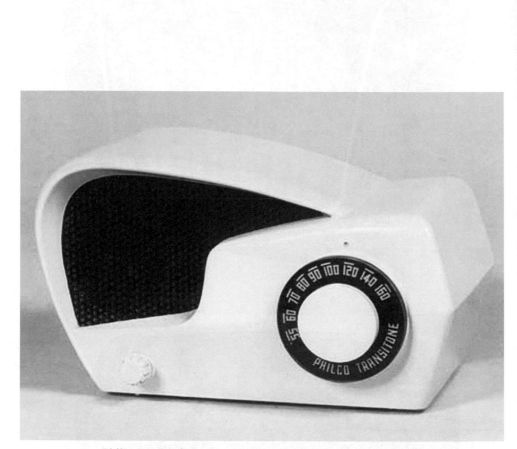

Philco Model 49501C - white 'boomerang' style radio, **$75-100**

Philco Model 46-420, front & back views, Bakelite, 1946, **$45-65**

Philco Model 38-15 wooden side table-style cabinet radio, 1938, **$100-150**

Packard Bell Model 5DA radio, front & back views, Bakelite, 1947, **$45-65**

Ogonyok 2 - front & back views, Russian, 1953, **$50-75**

Magnavox Model 155B console model---1948, **$75-100**

Keen Tone radio in dark plastic case w/slanted front right, grille at left, ca. 1939, **$75-100**

Jefferson Tube Rejuvenator--- circa 1930, **$20-30**

Howard FM Radio, 1948, **$25-50**

Firestone Model S74021---1939, Beetle plastic, **$100-150**
(note: the radio shown is cracked/damaged)

Esquire Model 517 lamp-radio with large shade, 1952, **$50-75**

Elimo "Jumbo Elim-O-Stat" interference eliminator with box, ca. 1930s-40s, **$25**

Bendix Model 526A radio in Bakelite case w/slide-rule dial at top, 1946, **$25-45**

Crosley Model 648, Blue plastic case, ca. 1940, **$50-75**

Crosley "Show Boy" model, 1931, repwood, **$350-500**

Crosley "The Pal" Colonial-style floor model console in a repwood cabinet,
front & back views, 1930, **$100-150**

Crosley "New Buddy" Model Radio with repwood cabinet, front & back views, 1930, **$200-250**

General Electric Model H520 - front view---1939, **$100-150**

INDEX